Sixty-Second Stewardship Sermons

Charles Cloughen, Jr.

A Liturgical Press Book

THE LITURGICAL PRESS
Collegeville, Minnesota

Cover design by Greg Becker

The author and publisher are grateful to Morehouse Publishing, Harrisburg, Pennsylvania, for permission to model *Sixty-Second Stewardship Sermons* on the Morehouse title *One-Minute Stewardship Sermons,* which was published in 1997.

3	4	5	6	7	8

Library of Congress Cataloging-in-Publication Data

Cloughen, Charles.
    Sixty-second stewardship sermons / Charles Cloughen, Jr.
       p.   cm.
    ISBN 0-8146-1219-9 (alk. paper)
    1. Stewardship, Christian—Sermons.   2. Sermons, American.
   3. Sermons, Spanish.   I. Title: 60-second stewardship sermons.
II. Title.

BV772.C575   2000
248'.6—dc21   99-054691
                                                       CIP

Contents

Foreword

In recent years, a new purpose has developed in many of our parishes—the idea of talking about stewardship at any time of year, at all times of year. Year-round stewardship has become a goal, not designed simply to increase giving to the Church, although this could not hurt, but rather, to recognize that stewardship lies at the very heart of Christian living and a Christian understanding of our possessions. Stewardship is about investing, an exciting concept for most of us because we expect a return. Our stewardship investing brings returns, as well, and they come out of our response to a loving God who has invested in us and in our Church.

Sixty-Second Stewardship Sermons is an excellent resource compiled by the Reverend Charles Cloughen, a priest of the Episcopal Diocese of Maryland in Baltimore, Maryland. The book itself makes the point that stewardship is in season in all seasons. There is no occasion and no Christian gathering in which a timely reminder of the importance of stewardship need be out of place. In fact, it is far more effective for pastors continuously to remind their parishioners of the importance and centrality of stewardship. How we invest what we have has a great deal to do with our spiritual well-being. Jesus makes this point in many of his parables and his other sayings. It can often be forgotten and, therefore, it is of even greater importance that we take seriously the effect that our material well-being has on our spiritual health. The people who feel spiritually whole are almost always those who have found exciting ways in which to invest their time, talent, and treasure, ways that bespeak their faith and the priorities that they hold dear. Such people are cheerful givers of themselves.

A central responsibility for pastors is to help to create a larger number of cheerful givers. *Sixty-Second Stewardship Sermons* is an excellent source of ideas on how stewardship can be communicated in a very short period of time on a regular basis, Sunday to Sunday, Solemnity to Solemnity, feast day to feast day.

What we have in the pages that follow is a practical resource to be used by pastors for the communication of stewardship at any time and all times of the year.

Most Reverend James Patrick Keleher, S.T.D.
Archbishop of Kansas City in Kansas
Episcopal Moderator of the International Catholic
Stewardship Council

Preface

Stewardship is Thanksgiving. It is giving thanks for all God has given us: all of our time, our talents, and our treasure. Stewardship is how we manage our entire lives and includes what we give back to God for God's work throughout the church. Sixty-second stewardship sermons may be incorporated into the regular sermon at Mass or printed in the bulletin, but they are primarily designed to stand alone and be given at the time of the Preparation of the Gifts.

With these stewardship sermons, through a hundred different illustrations, stewardship leaders in the Catholic and ecumenical churches connect the mission and vision of the local church with the stewardship of the church members' time, talent, and treasure. These sermons will be especially effective for the "Boomers," the "X-Generation," and the un-churched or newly churched members.

The sermons are organized: first, in a general way, by Scripture; second, by certain Sundays and Solemnities of the church year; and third, by topic. They are offered as illustrations of how one can make use of stewardship sermons in the context of the Eucharist. They are cross-indexed in the appendix.

Acknowledgments

I once heard of a person who, when he was honored for his accomplishments, responded: "I stood on the shoulders of giants!" That is the way I feel regarding this book, *Sixty-Second Stewardship Sermons*. I am standing on the shoulders of so many others and benefiting from their vision, passion, and teaching.

My good friend and colleague Robert Daly taught me a wonderful quotation: "All great ideas normally degenerate into hard work."

This book would not have been possible without the hard work and help of:

My wife Judy, whose love, encouragement, support, and understanding enabled me to write this book.

Elizabeth Huntress, my mother-in-law, who was my patient and hardworking primary editor and who prepared the final draft.

The parishioners of Saint Thomas' Church, where I have been serving as pastor since 1990. They generously gave me time to attend the Second International Stewardship Conference in Rome in 1998 and to develop this book on stewardship.

Matthew R. Paratore, Secretary General of the International Catholic Stewardship Council, Inc., Washington, D.C., without whose help, support, and guidance this book could not have been written.

My special thanks goes to those who accepted my invitation to be readers for *Sixty-Second Stewardship Sermons*. They helped me better to understand the Catholic mind and viewpoint.

John Capobianco, President   '
Lumen Catechetical Consultants, Inc.
Silver Spring, Maryland

Rev. Msgr. Joseph Champlin, Rector
Cathedral of the Immaculate Conception
Syracuse, New York

Most Rev. Robert Morneau, Auxiliary Bishop
Diocese of Green Bay, Wisconsin

Edward Laughlin, Director of Stewardship
Diocese of Palm Beach, Florida

Introduction

Have you ever heard of Crest®? I believe that if a person asked one hundred people this question, ninety-eight would reply, "Sure! You mean Crest® toothpaste." Why does Procter & Gamble® spend millions of dollars a year to tell us about Crest® by offering brief commercials frequently throughout the year? If they really want to get their message out, why don't they buy a half-hour block of prime time television to tell the Crest® story?

This simple illustration from the secular world helps to teach us something about stewardship. Church members pledge and give for the ministry of the church and not to pay parish bills or to reduce a deficit, in the same way that they buy Crest® to protect their teeth, not to help pay bills for Procter & Gamble®. Loading an entire yearly stewardship message into one annual twenty-minute stewardship sermon is equivalent to Proctor & Gamble®'s loading their entire yearly advertising message into one commercial in the fall.

There is a better way.

In many Christian churches, a most awkward moment comes before and during the Preparation of the Gifts. Many clergy and other leaders of worship ignore this moment to teach and miss the chance every week to continue stewardship education at an opportune point in the service. The bringing forward of the gifts and the time used in preparing the elements for Communion are a natural lead-in to stewardship education. I often suggest this concept to other clergy, saying, "There is a way to make use of these awkward moments—the stewardship sermon. Try one; you might be pleasantly surprised." And they have found that the suggestion works.

My epiphany came some twenty years ago during an Episcopal Stewardship Conference in Attelboro, Massachusetts, sponsored by the Episcopal Church's National Stewardship Office. At this workshop, one speaker, the Rev. George Regas, pastor of All Saints Episcopal Church, Pasadena, California, mentioned what he did at the Offertory. He explained to us that he talked about money (stating that the clergy are accused of doing that anyway) and used this time to explain the ministry that was being done by the church with the money that the members pledged and gave each week.

Over these past twenty years I have worked to expand his ideas and to develop the concept of connecting money and ministry in the area of stewardship and planned giving. During the majority of the services I give one of my sixty-second stewardship sermons, connecting what each person and family gives— in the way of time, talents, and treasure—with the ministry of the church. I do this in the spirit of thanksgiving, rather than begging. It transforms the Offertory into a time of joy and thanksgiving for God's gifts given to us. I connect these stewardship sermons to our mission and vision, which, at St. Thomas' Church, is to worship and serve in Jesus' name.

This time of teaching, week by week, is crucial if we are to educate the hearts and minds of the "Boomers," the "Generation Xers," the "Busters," and the newly churched members on the principles and practices of giving. The future of our churches depends on the conversion of the these generations to a generation of those who give generously of their time, talents, and treasure to God's work that is being accomplished through the greater church. Their future depends on their realizing the need to give generously of themselves, sharing what they have with others in the building of a Christian community.

One of the greatest challenges for the church (parish or diocesan) is communicating its mission and vision. In my congregation, I know that if I place a notice of an event in the monthly newsletter, in the Sunday bulletin, and on our two bulletin boards, about 50 percent of the church members will remember and know it is happening. In the twenty-first century, a church that relies merely on the written word will be in trouble.

"Sixty-Second Stewardship Sermons" are designed to help meet the challenge the Catholic church faces in the twenty-first century in communicating stewardship to those under fifty, many of whom have no history of *duty* to the church. Experience has taught me that people enter the church (the unchurched who have never been members of a church and who are totally unfamiliar with church tradition) or reenter the church (the dischurched who at some time in their lives attended church, and who, after an absence, are returning to attend regularly) at low giving levels. Then, if good stewardship teaching takes place, they increase their giving to support the mission and vision of the local and greater church. I believe this increase comes out of their God-given need to give. They will not support the parish merely out of duty, and so the local parish cannot thrive unless there is solid stewardship education. Also, appealing merely to people to give to reduce the deficit or to meet the budget offers little or no attraction, either for these new givers or for our regular congregation. In itself, the need of the church to survive has little appeal for anyone.

Our local parishes have to develop a solid mission and vision and communicate this vision week by week so that the worshipers will be eager to give of their time, talent, and treasure to make that vision happen. The Catholic Church, if it is going to thrive and prosper, needs to build and then communicate a mission and vision that will move local parishes, the parish council, and the general membership to give their time, talent, and treasure to support the larger vision and mission. Local parishes will respond with their stewardship appeals for local mission initiatives such as food pantries, soup kitchens, and shelters for abused women and pregnant teenagers. In many cases, these projects are ecumenically based.

In the Episcopal Church, we sometimes practice a pairing of congregations. In our diocese, the strategy for the twenty-first century is the pairing of affluent suburban congregations with inner-city congregations, sharing resources to "make disciples of all nations." This is not following the old model of merely sending money to missions, but a true partnership—exchanging choirs and clergy—creating a true two-way street. In the Archdiocese of Baltimore, a pairing of suburban and inner-city parochial schools is being developed as a way of encouraging better understanding. Concepts such as these will give the church goer of the twenty-first century excellent hands-on ministry opportunities.

The teaching of stewardship is actually the making of faithful disciples of Jesus Christ. These stewardship sermons are designed to be used to thank people for their part in making good things happen—not only talking about the future but also acknowledging their support of time, talent, and treasure, week after week, in making possible the many ministries that our local churches are providing.

Sixty-Second Stewardship Sermons was created by taking a personal theology of stewardship and connecting it to the mission and vision of the ministry of the congregation or institution we serve, when we *thank* the people for what they have *already* accomplished by giving of their time, abilities, and money.

This book deals first with building a theological foundation based on biblical theology and stewardship—a foundation based on abundance not scarcity, a foundation based on an appreciation of God's abundant gifts that we have already received. Second, it deals with guidelines on how best to construct these sermons. The third major section offers examples written by outstanding stewardship leaders from both the Catholic Church and from many other denominations, which may be used as written or serve as inspiration in writing one's own stewardship sermons.

This book is written from my own experiences as a pastor in the Episcopal Church. However, I hope it will be helpful for all in the Catholic community who want to work for stronger stewardship. To help make the concepts in this book more easily understood by everyone, some terms are defined.

First, the head clergy person in the Catholic Church is called a pastor. Most clergy who fulfill a pastoral function are priests, assisted by deacons, religious, and lay persons.

The parish/pastoral council is the term for a parish's advisory board within the life of the parish. In the past, the parish was defined as a geographic area of the church's local ministry, but now, many parishioners cross over to other parishes to worship in a church that they believe better meets their needs.

Catholic churches belong to a diocese, a geographical area that normally is named after a city—the Archdiocese of Baltimore, for example. The head of the diocese is the bishop appointed by the Holy Father, the Pope. In the United States the Catholic Church has an association of bishops called the National Conference of Catholic Bishops.

I hope you will find this book helpful, whether you are a pastor, a worship presider, a stewardship chairman, a member of a stewardship committee, the development committee, finance committee, a liturgical minister, a member of the parish or pastoral council, or a faithful member of a church concerned about your own and your church's stewardship.

The Rev. Charles Cloughen, Jr.

1

Developing Your Theology of Stewardship

Do you really believe that God will provide for you and your family's needs? In the Sermon on the Mount, Jesus tells us:

> "Give and gifts will be given to you; a good measure, packed together, shaken down, and overflowing, will be poured into your lap. For the measure with which you measure will in return be measured out to you" (Luke 6:38).

God is generous, giving, loving, forgiving, and gracious. God desires our loving response to God's generosity. In reading books on stewardship, what stands out for me is the personal witness of the writer, who has been the recipient of God's generosity. I have not always given generously to God through the church, but my wife Judy and I have been generously blessed. God's generosity can be seen most clearly in retrospect. Examine your life. Search to see God's generous hand in it. Take out a pad of paper and write down the times in your life or in the lives of others close to you when God's hand has been present. Ponder these examples. They will make wonderful illustrations for your stewardship teaching and preaching.

Now think of some times when your parish has stepped out in faith and God has been there. Jot down those times and save them; they too will be wonderful stewardship sermons.

When we have acted faithfully and *responsively,* God has provided. A quotation from the Rev. Sara Chandler, adjunct professor of stewardship at the Virginia Theological Seminary, states: "God doesn't order what God won't pay for!"

Stewardship is a way of life, giving thanks for all that God has given us—our time, our talents, and our treasure. Stewardship is the way we manage *all* our time, talents, and treasure. Nothing of value happens in human life without these three currencies. Nothing of value happens in the life of a church without these three currencies. Some think of stewardship as what we give, or return, to God for God's work through the church; they teach that the tithe means 10 percent of our worldly goods. I believe that 100 percent is God's.

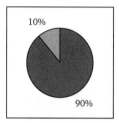

90% Ours
10% God's Work

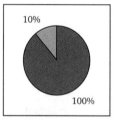

100% God's
10% God's Work

Our stewardship is our decision as to how we live and manage our entire life. What we return to God through the church is only a part of our stewardship. We are given by God the freedom to manage all of our time, talents, and treasure. We strive to discern the mind of Christ as we work to become the hands of Christ.

Are You a Good Steward?

The first key to good stewardship in a congregation is the pastor.

1. Is the pastor comfortable about money?

2. Does the pastor pledge?

3. Does the pastor tithe?

4. Is the pastor comfortable about preaching and teaching about money and tithing?

Is Tithing Christian? Is It Biblical?

If one examines the Hebrew Scriptures, one finds many explanations of tithes and offerings. In Genesis, Abram is blessed by Melchizedek after he brings his tithe to the priest.

> When Abram returned from his victory over Chedorlaomer and the kings who were allied with him, the king of Sodom went out to greet him at the Valley of Shaveh (that is, the King's Valley).
>
> Melchizedek, king of Salem, brought out bread and wine, and being a priest of God Most High, he blessed Abram with these words:
>
> "Blessed be Abram by God Most High,
>   the creator of heaven and earth;
> And blessed be God Most High,
>   who delivered your foes into your hand" (Gen 14:17-20).

In Deuteronomy 14 the Hebrews are told to set aside a tithe of their harvest to give thanks to God in a wonderful celebration of Thanksgiving:

> "Each year you shall tithe all the produce that grows in the field you have sown; then, in the place that the LORD, your God, chooses as the dwelling place of his name, you shall eat in his presence your tithe of the grain, wine and oil, as well as the firstlings of your herd and flock, that you may learn always to fear the LORD your God. If, however, the journey is too much for you, and you are not able to bring your tithe, because the place which the LORD, your God, chooses for the abode of his name is too far for you, considering how the LORD has blessed you, you may exchange the tithe for money, and with the purse of money in hand, go to the place which the LORD, your God, chooses. You may then exchange the money for whatever you desire, oxen or sheep, wine or strong drink, or anything else you would enjoy, and there before the LORD, your God, you shall partake of it and make merry with your family. But do not neglect the Levite

who belongs to your community, for he has no share in the heritage with you.

"At the end of every third year you shall bring out all the tithes of your produce for that year and deposit them in community stores, that the Levite who has no share in the heritage with you, and also the alien, the orphan and the widow who belong to your community, may come and eat their fill; so that the LORD, your God, may bless you in all that you undertake" (Deut 14:22-29).

In chapter 26, the Hebrews set aside a tithe every third year for the Levites, aliens, orphans, and widows, those who are in need:

"When you have finished setting aside all the tithes of your produce in the third year, the year of the tithes, and you have given them to the Levite, the alien, the orphan and the widow, that they may eat their fill in your own community, you shall declare before the LORD, your God: "I have purged my house of the sacred portion and I have given it to the Levite, the alien, the orphan and the widow, just as you have commanded me. In this I have not broken or forgotten any of your commandments: I have not eaten any of the tithe as a mourner; I have not brought any of it out as one unclean; I have not offered any of it to the dead. I have thus hearkened to the voice of the LORD, my God, doing just as you commanded me" (Deut 26:12-14).

In Malachi, God speaks to the Hebrews in the way of rebuke to those who have not returned their tithe:

Since the days of your fathers, you have turned aside
  from my statutes and have not kept them.
Return to me, and I will return to you,
  says the LORD of hosts.
Yet you say, "How must we return?"
  Dare a man rob God? Yet you are robbing me!
And you say, "How do we rob you?"
  In tithes and offerings!
You are indeed accursed,
  for you, the whole nation, rob me!
Bring the whole tithe
  into the storehouse,

That there may be food in my house,
   and try me in this, says the LORD of hosts:
Shall I not open for you the floodgates of heaven,
   To pour down blessing upon you without measure?
For your sake I will forbid the locust to destroy your crops;
And the vine in the field shall not be barren,
   says the LORD of hosts.
Then all nations will call you blessed
   for you will be a delightful,
   says the LORD of hosts (Mal 3:7-12).

In the Hebrew Scriptures, wealth was viewed as a sign of God's blessings and the presentation of tithes was expected as a sign of our thankfulness for these blessings. Moses, David, Solomon, and Job were all blessed by God in a material way. But they were expected to return tithes (10 percent of their income, produce, wheat, animals, goats, wine, etc.) to care for the Temple and the poor.

Jesus and Money

In reading the Gospels, it is clear that tithing was the standard of giving for the Jews at the time of Jesus. Jesus takes tithing for granted, but warns us against making the tithe an idol, about becoming prideful about it and substituting it for compassion.

Woe to you Pharisees! You pay tithes of mint and of rue and of every garden herb, but you pay no attention to judgment and to love for God. These you should have done, without overlooking the others (Luke 11:42).

Jesus gave this illustration after observing how much people were giving at the Temple in Jerusalem. (And you think Jesus does not care how much we put in the collection basket?)

When he looked up he saw some wealthy people putting their offerings into the treasury and he noticed a poor widow put in two small coins. He said, "I tell you truly, this poor widow put in more than all the rest; for those others have all made offerings from their surplus wealth, but she, from her poverty, has offered her whole livelihood" (Luke 21:1-4).

The widow who gave everything was held up for praise. When I have discussed tithing with governing boards, inevitably someone, usually a man who has a good job and income, will say: "Remember the widow's mite." I have responded, "In the New Testament, there is no gift too large in thanksgiving for the kingdom of God. If you want to give all you have, as she did, it will be gratefully accepted." (Obviously, that is not exactly what he had in mind.) As North American Christians, we resemble more the rich giving from our abundance rather than the widow from her scarcity. Overall, I have found widows to be generous in their giving to God through their church. Jesus knows us as we know our own brothers and sisters.

The standard of the widow's mite is observed in monasteries and convents, where, when members accept the life of poverty, chastity, and obedience, they give all their income and assets to the order—truly, "all they have."

Jesus has more to say about us and our possessions (our wealth) than about any other subject of our spiritual life. He tells us:

> "Do not be afraid any longer, little flock, for your Father is pleased to give you the kingdom. Sell your belongings and give alms. Provide money bags for yourselves that do not wear out, an inexhaustible treasure in heaven that no thief can reach nor moth destroy. For where your treasure is, there also will your heart be" (Luke 12:32-34).

The value of the kingdom of God requires everything. Our possessions—our house, cars, clothes, and computers—are not going to make it to heaven. We must leave those behind for others. Only *people* are going to heaven. Through the god of materialism, our world tells us to use people to acquire money and wealth to buy things. Jesus calls us to do the opposite: give and invest in our children, our young people, our adults. *Love people and use things!*

Jesus knew well the value of money and the power of wealth. In the parable of the talents (Matt 25:14-30), a man gives to three servants (slaves) five, two, and one talent each. Jesus is talking about trusting these slaves with real money. For these

slaves, "each talent was worth fifteen years of wages as a la-
borer" (NRSV). Today, if one is paid the current minimum wage
over the course of fifteen years, the equivalent of one talent
would be $132,600. We really should read this passage as: "The
master gave to one servant $633,000, to one $265,200, and to
one $132,600." Now that is real money. That gets our atten-
tion. The two who doubled their money were told,

> "Well done, my good and faithful servant. Since you were
> faithful in small matters, I will give you great responsibili-
> ties. Come, share your master's joy" (Matt 25:23).

I believe that individually and corporately we are supposed
to risk and invest in the kingdom of Heaven. I often see the
church not acting as the first two servants did—risking and investing in the kingdom of God—but acting like the third servant, hoarding, afraid it will lose what God has given it.

In the church there is a saying, "When is a business person
not a business person? When that person is a member of the
parish/pastoral council." A corollary would be, "When are priests
not missionaries? When they preside at parish/pastoral council
meetings." I have constantly seen business men and women who
take risks in business, risks in personal investment, and then, as
members of the council, act timidly, afraid of risking and using
God's money. I have seen clergy who expound great vision, but,
when chairing a meeting, act out of self interest to protect the
parish.

Jesus warns us about the power of possession, money, and
wealth in the parable of the rich man:

> As he [Jesus] was setting out on a journey, a man ran up,
> knelt down before him, and asked him, "Good teacher, what
> must I do to inherit eternal life?" Jesus answered him, "Why
> do you call me good? No one is good but God alone. You
> know the commandments: 'You shall not kill; you shall not
> commit adultery; you shall not steal; you shall not bear
> false witness; you shall not defraud; honor your father and
> your mother.'" He replied and said to him, "Teacher, all of
> these I have observed from my youth." Jesus, looking at
> him, loved him and said to him, "You are lacking in one

thing. Go, sell what you have, and give to [the] poor and
you will have treasure in heaven; then come, follow me." At
that statement, his face fell, and he went away sad, for he
had many possessions (Mark 10:17-22).

"Jesus looking at him, loved him." What a wonderful image
of Jesus looking into the man's eyes and loving him and invit-
ing him to be a disciple. All he had to do was sell his possessions and give them to the poor. What an adventure he was
offered, life with Jesus. Today, there would be numerous churches
named after him—his name would be known along with the
names of Peter, Thomas, Mark, and John; instead, he walked
away grieving, no name, walking into obscurity with all his
possessions, worshipping the god of money and materialism. It
is clear that discipleship requires the commitment of our time,
talents, and treasure if we are to follow Jesus Christ.

The last Scripture passage I cite concerning the words and
teaching of Jesus on money and possessions is from Matthew:

No one can serve two masters. He will either hate one and
love the other, or be devoted to one and despise the other.
You cannot serve God and mammon (Matt 6:24).

Each one of us must choose and keep choosing the master we
will serve—God or mammon (wealth). In his *The Challenge of
the Disciplined Life,* Richard Foster deals with the power of mammon—money. It is not neutral; it has power to control and cor-
rupt the creatures of God or be used for great good. He states:

What all this talk about stewardship fails to see is that money
is not just a neutral medium of exchange but a "power" with
a life of its own. And very often it is a "power" that is de-
monic in character. As long as we think of money in imper-
sonal terms alone, no moral problems exist aside from the
proper use of it. But when we begin to take seriously the
Biblical perspective that money is animated and energized
by "powers" then our relationship to money is filled with
moral consequence (p. 24).

Our relationship to money is what concerns God. Whom do we
worship? What do we worship?

Paul and Money

In 2 Corinthians Paul tells us about the early church's understanding of money, how it is shared and given to the saints in Jerusalem. He encourages us to be generous:

> Consider this: whoever sows sparingly will also reap sparingly, and whoever sows bountifully will also reap bountifully. Each must do as already determined, without sadness or compulsion, for God loves a cheerful giver. Moreover, God is able to make every grace abundant for you, so that in all things, always having all you need, you may have an abundance for every good work (2 Cor 9:6-8).

We are to give cheerfully out of our abundance, not as the world gives grudgingly out of its scarcity. Thus the early church saw itself abundantly blessed with money, sharing God's blessings of money, with the "saints in Jerusalem."

The church's history of stewardship, its use and teachings of our time, abilities, and money from the days of Paul and the early church, to Constantine—the age of Christendom, to our time in the nineties—post Christendom, would take a book in itself.

Today we face, as the church and its people have always faced, the power of mammon—money. All around us we are confronted with the god of materialism. A perfect example of this worship of mammon is found in a huge new mall in Towson, Maryland. One walks into this secular cathedral to an atrium four stories high, all open to the ceiling, with waterfalls, sculptures of angels, chairs on which to meditate on the abundance of the god of materialism, classical piano music to inspire the soul, a wonderful dome rivaling St. Peter's in Rome—all this to meet your every need:

- Depressed about your marriage? Buy a new suit—just charge it to your American Express® card.

- Anxious about your job? Buy a pair of designer shoes—just charge them to your Discover® card.

- Afraid of being alone? Buy a forty-inch television with remote control to keep you company. Just charge it to your Visa® card. You won't even have to move from your

La-ZBoy® chair to change the thirty-five channels on your cable.

- Unhappy? Buy a diamond tennis bracelet and charge it to Mastercard®.
- Overweight and slothful? Buy a NordicTrack® to bring back your youth. Just write a check and bring your balance down to zero.

The god of materialism has a solution for your every problem. On any Sunday afternoon, it is impossible to find a parking space in the mall's seven-floor parking garage. If a Martian were to look down at Earth, he would indeed see the shopping mall, with its acres of parking lots and hordes of people coming and going in all directions, as our cathedral to the god of money!

The only way we can confront money's power of possessiveness is by giving it away freely and cheerfully, from the wonderful blessings we have received from God.

The words of Jesus still ring in my ears, flash before my eyes, and cause my heart to race: "For where your treasure is, there also your heart will be" (Luke 12:34.) We need to be vigilant and watchful of our treasure (money). There is a wonderful story that speaks to our earthly and heavenly treasure:

> Miss Mary Clark was the wealthiest woman in the Virginia town of Clarkesville. Never married, she lived alone, in a mansion on top of the highest hill in town. She attended church occasionally, although she never pledged—believed in a "freewill offering." Driven by her chauffeur, she attended church every Christmas, Easter, and Pentecost. When the plate was passed, she would proudly put her crisp new $100 bill on top of the collection. But that was all she ever gave. When the new parochial school wing was being built at the church, the parish council came to her for a major gift; they w trying to raise $200,000 for the project. She knew there were two hundred giving units, so, afraid of being taken advantage of, she gave her share of $1,000 and was proud of it. When the new library was being built in town, she gave $100 and was insulted when nothing was named after her. At age 84, God called her home. Her estate of $5,000,000 went to a distant niece,

whom she had last seen twenty years ago and who was married to a heart surgeon.

When she arrived in heaven, St. Peter picked her up in the heavenly bus to take her to her new home. She drove past mansions, which she thought were fitting for a person of her station; she was shocked to see her kind and generous maid, one of the most giving members of her community, living in one of them. The bus kept going, passing through a section of modest houses—one occupied by a teacher from the parochial high school; rowhouses—occupied by her childhood pastor; and down a dirt road to a ramshackle house with no doors or windows and an unfinished roof. Miss Mary Clark was indignant. In her best upper-class pride, she asked, "What is the meaning of this outrage?" St. Peter responded, "This is the best we could do with what you sent up!"

What are you and the members of your congregation sending up to heaven?

The Roman Catholic Stewardship Story

We are living in a world where, for many, their "god" is materialism, where human beings are judged by their yearly income and net worth. The world says, "Accumulate! Have! Hoard!" We say, "Share! Give cheerfully to God's work through the church!"

We have been given wisdom by God, we are teachable, we can learn what God is calling his servants to be and to give in our time. Our experience tells us that stewardship works—it enables us to confront the god of our age—the god of materialism.

Each Sunday, as we gather to worship and serve in Jesus' name, remembering our model, Mary, the Mother of Jesus, these *Sixty-Second Stewardship Sermons* help communicate the relationship between the mission and vision of the parish, and the faithful stewardship of each parishioner and each household's use of time, talent, and treasure.

Parishioners do not give just to meet the budget of the church, but to further the ministry of the parish, the diocese, the world. They do not give to pay utility bills (although they realize that these have to be paid), but to provide light and heat in order that we may worship in the church, to assure warm, well-lighted places where children can get to know Jesus, and where parish groups can meet to learn and be healed. They give so that the sick may be healed, the world may know Jesus—and that they may have a place in which to offer their prayers and receive the sacraments, especially to receive the body and blood of Christ.

Most of our pastors and bishops received little or no training in stewardship during their seminary training for the priesthood. So often, their only stewardship experience was dealing with the need to ask for more money to pay the bills or taking collections for missionary work. Our laity were taught to pray, pay, and obey.

In 1962, the National Catholic Stewardship Council, Inc., Washington, D.C., was formed to educate Catholics about stewardship as a way of life. In his address at the First International NCSC Conference in Rome on October 11, 1973, Pope Paul VI complimented Catholic stewardship:

> You are striving to draw from the concept of stewardship all the richness of meaning which this term implies in the Gospel, and to show the value of offering to God, as an act of worship, part of the gifts received from his bounty.*

> **A Brief History of the National Catholic Stewardship Council, Inc.* (1997).

Throughout the past twenty-seven years the Council has worked to present stewardship, not as a way to raise money, but instead, as a way of life walking with Jesus, based on the example of Mary, Mother of Jesus, who said yes to God. Stewardship is how we manage all our time, talent, and treasure as God's gifts to us.

In 1993, the NCSC adopted a definition of stewardship:

> Stewardship is a complete lifestyle, a life of total accountability and responsibility acknowledging God as creator and owner of all. Stewards as disciples of Jesus Christ see themselves as caretakers of all God's gifts. Gratitude for these gifts is expressed in prayer, worship, offering, and action only by sharing these gifts out of love for one another.

Today, we find the best theological, Catholic pillars of stewardship in "To Be A Christian Steward," a summary of the U.S.

Bishops Pastoral Letter entitled *Stewardship. A Disciple's Response,* approved by the National Conference of Catholic Bishops, November 1992.

I have graciously been given permission to publish a summary of this fine document from the United States Catholic Conference, but I urge every pastor, pastoral/parish council, stewardship, and development committee to order a full text available both in Spanish and English from the United States Catholic Conference, Washington, D.C. 20017 (1-800-235-8722).

To Be a Christian Steward

A Summary of the U.S. Bishops' Pastoral Letter on Stewardship*

As each one has received a gift, use it to serve one another as good stewards of God's varied grace (1 Pet 4:10).

What identifies a steward? Safeguarding material and human resources and using them responsibly are one answer; so is generous giving of time, talent, and treasure. But being a Christian steward means more. As Christian stewards, we receive God's gifts gratefully, cultivate them responsibly, share them lovingly in justice with others, and return them with increase to the Lord.

Disciples as Stewards

Let us begin with being a disciple—a follower of our Lord Jesus Christ. As members of the Church, Jesus calls us to be disciples. This has astonishing implications:

—Mature disciples make a conscious decision to follow Jesus, no matter what the cost.

—Christian disciples experience conversion—life shaping changes of mind and heart—and commit their very selves to the Lord.

*Reprinted with permission of the National Conference of Catholic Bishops, Washington, D.C. 20017.

—Christian stewards respond in a particular way to the call to be a disciple. Stewardship has the power to shape and mold our understanding of our lives and the way in which we live.

Jesus' disciples and Christian stewards recognize God as the origin of life, giver of freedom, and source of all things. We are grateful for the gifts we have received and are eager to use them to show our love for God and for one another. We look to the life and teaching of Jesus for guidance in living as Christian stewards.

Stewards of Creation

The Bible contains a profound message about the stewardship of material creation: God created the world, but entrusts it to human beings. Caring for and cultivating the world involves the following:

—joyful appreciation for the God-given beauty and wonder of nature;

—protection and preservation of the environment, which would be the stewardship of ecological concern;

—respect for human life—shielding life from threat and assault, doing everything that can be done to enhance this gift and make life flourish; and

—development of this world through noble human effort—physical labor, the trades and professions, the arts and sciences. We call such effort work.

Work is a fulfilling human vocation. The Second Vatican Council points out that, through work, we build up not only our world but the kingdom of God, already present among us. Work as partnership with God—our share in a divine-human collaboration in creation. It occupies a central place in our lives as Christian stewards.

Stewards of Vocation

Jesus calls us, as his disciples, to a new way of life—the Christian way of life—of which stewardship is part.

But Jesus does not call us as nameless people in a faceless crowd. He calls us individually, by name. Each one of us—clergy, religious, lay person; married, single; adult, child—has a personal vocation. God intends each one of us to play a unique role in carrying out the divine plan.

The challenge, then, is to understand our role—our vocation—and to respond generously to this call from God. Christian vocation entails the practice of stewardship. In addition, Christ calls each of us to be stewards of our personal vocations, which we receive from God.

Stewards of the Church

Stewards of God's gifts are not passive beneficiaries. We cooperate with God in our own redemption and in the redemption of others. We are also obliged to be stewards of the Church—collaborators and cooperators in continuing the redemptive work of Jesus Christ, which is the Church's essential mission. This mission—proclaiming and teaching, serving and sanctifying—is our task. It is the personal responsibility of each one of us as stewards of the Church.

All members of the Church have their own roles to play in carrying out its mission.

—parents, who nurture their children in the light of faith;

—parishioners, who work in concrete ways to make their parishes true communities of faith and vibrant sources of service to the larger community;

—all Catholics, who give generous support—time, money, prayer, and personal service according to their circumstances—to parish and diocesan programs and to the universal Church.

Obstacles to Stewardship

People who want to live as Christian disciples and Christian stewards face serious obstacles.

In the United States and other nations, a dominant secular culture often contradicts religious convictions about the meaning of life. This culture frequently encourages us to focus on ourselves and our pleasures. At times, we can find it far too easy to ignore spiritual realities and to deny religion a role in shaping human and social values.

As Catholics who have entered into the mainstream of American society and experienced its advantages, many of us also have been adversely influenced by this secular culture. We know what it is to struggle against selfishness and greed, and we realize that it is harder for many today to accept the challenge of being a Christian steward.

It is essential, therefore, that we make a special effort to understand the true meaning of stewardship and live accordingly.

A Steward's Way

The life of a Christian steward models the life of Jesus. It is challenging and even difficult, in many respects, yet intense joy comes to those who take the risk to live as Christian stewards. Women and men who seek to live as stewards learn that "all things work for good for those who love God" (Rom 8:28).

After Jesus, we look to Mary as an ideal steward. As the Mother of Christ, she lived her ministry in a spirit of fidelity and service; she responded generously to the call.

We must ask ourselves: Do we also wish to be disciples of Jesus Christ and Christian stewards of our world and our Church?

Central to our human and Christian vocations, as well as to the unique vocation each one of us receives from God, is that we be good stewards of the gifts we possess. God gives us this divine–human workshop, this world and Church of ours.

The Spirit shows us the way.

Stewardship is part of that journey.

———————————————————————

Stewardship. A Disciple's Response is a pastoral letter on stewardship in six parts. Each section is followed by discussion questions for appropriate parish/pastoral council, stewardship committee, or theology study groups. This pastoral letter is the foundation for all diocesan and parish stewardship programs.

The letter is a treasure that many pastors, parish councils, pastoral councils leave buried in the pastor's study or parish library.

Stewardship in many Catholics' minds, when they hear the word stewardship, spell it $tewardship. I spell S✝ewardship with a cross. Our Catholic Bishops emphasize stewardship as *a way of life,* with Jesus at the center and Mary as the ideal model of the steward. Mary said "Yes!" to God, bore God's son, and practiced a life of sacrifice.

Through our teaching and preaching we can excite our parishioners about how thankful we are to be invited to be a part of God's plan and work and how we can return to God a part of what God has given each of us.

Many parishes have members who know how to organize, support, and raise money—lots of money. These parishioners constantly work and organize fundraising through Bingo, 50-50s, dances, and the like for the United Way, soccer and little league teams, private and parochial schools, the Democratic and Republican Parties, and myriads of local charities. What is lacking for the church is not organizational skills for fundraising, but a theology of giving—a biblical theology of stewardship based on the Bishops' Pastoral Letter. There are wonderful nuts-and-bolts plans on how to conduct an effective stewardship program, but *always* the weak point for our parishioners is a lack of stewardship theology. This cannot be taught in just one sermon a year, but must be developed slowly, week by week, through repetitive, low-key experiences, like these sixty-second stewardship sermons.

Too frequently in our preaching we focus only on the challenge and commitment of giving. In *Giving and Stewardship in an Effective Church,* Kennon Callahan defines what motivates people to give and believes that "the grassroots and unchurched" are moved to give by compassion and community, values appealed to by these sermons. On a week-to-week basis they communicate with everyone, the not-yet churched and the grassroots, as well as those who have accepted the challenge and are committed already to a stewardship of time, talent, and treasure.

The stewardship sermons are an important part of my Sunday worship service. Preceding the taking of the offering, I preach one sixty-second sermon from memory. I believe that the giving of the offering—ourselves—is our response to Jesus' sacrifice for us.

I consider this "mini-sermon" as important as the full sermon or homily I share each Sunday with the parish. When the offering has been received, we need a way to celebrate our parishioners' offering of themselves represented by their generous gifts given at Mass, what God has given us. In the Episcopal Church, *The Book of Common Prayer* directs that the offerings be presented and placed on the altar. In the Roman Catholic tradition I suggest that a large basket with the offering be placed at the foot of the altar. In this way we honor those who have given freely by the way we treat their gifts. So often, the Sunday offering is looked upon as an unpleasant necessity to be quickly whisked away out of sight, rather than a visible and joyful expression of a way of life.

We are a church rich in symbolic meaning. In the Catholic Church the liturgy is an experience in sight, sound, and sensation. What we do visually with the offering is as important as what we say about it. Our parishioners need to experience the joy of giving.

We as clergy and members of our parishes need to examine our budgets and ministries by Jesus' standards. The money sitting in front of our altar, freely given, is made sacred to God's work in God's world—to change that world for which Jesus gave his life.

All ministry of clergy—religious and laity—and of all who are baptized make up stewardship. God has made us holy. This includes our time, our talents, and our treasure. Today, we need models for discipleship such as those presented to us by Dr. Andrew Simone and his wife Joan who were awarded the N.C.S.C., Inc., Christian Stewards' Award for their feeding hungry children by founding of the Canadian Food for Children Organization.

Mary, the Mother of Jesus, said "Yes!" to God as she loved and cherished her son Jesus Christ. Today, she is called the Mother of God because she said and lived her "Yes!" When we practice responsible stewardship of our time, talent, and treasure, we too are saying yes by responding to God's love and generosity.

As Bishop Morneau, auxiliary bishop of Green Bay, Wisconsin, states: "We need to celebrate the JOY—the tremendous joy that comes from a life of gospel generosity." We need to be aware that to accept the stewardship way of life is risky; it means overcoming the fear of not having enough. Bishop Morneau reminds me of "the need to pray for *trust* and the need for *trust* and the support of others."

Money has incredible power to do good or evil. We believe that the power can be harnessed for good—to fulfill Jesus' mission when he speaks of how we will be judged as a person and as a church, as stated in Matt 25:34-36:

> "Come, you who are blessed by my Father. Inherit the kingdom prepared for you from the foundation of the world. For I was hungry and you gave me food, I was thirsty and you gave me drink, a stranger and you welcomed me, naked and you clothed me, ill and you cared for me, in prison and you visited me."

The Future of Stewardship Throughout the World

In December 1998, the Second International Stewardship Seminar was held in Rome, sponsored by the NCSC with the title: "Stewardship for Global Solidarity." Stewardship leaders from around the world participated in the conference, and I was honored to be the representative of the Episcopal Church, U.S.A.

In our audience with Pope John Paul II, he said, "I extend a warm welcome to the National Catholic Stewardship Council. I thank you for your efforts to increase awareness among the faithful for their responsibility for the church's mission."

We all left our five-day seminar in Rome with a strong sense of the mission of the church as we enter the twenty-first century.

On December 8 we experienced the highlight of our worship experience when the Solemnity of the Immaculate Conception was celebrated at the Church of Santa Susanna in Rome. The celebrant and homilist of this Mass was Pio Cardinal Laghi, Prefect of Congregation for Catholic Education. The cardinal reminded us that "Mary is not only present at the beginning of the history of our redemption, she is also present before us, as a model of sanctity and grace . . . a model of virtue, the advocate of grace and forgiveness, the Star that safely guides us across the threshold of the Third Millennium full of hope and good intentions. . . ." (NCSC *Resource,* 1999).

At this conference, my perception was that three major challenges were presented to the Catholic Church in the twenty-first century:

1) the interdenominational connection between Evangelization and Stewardship;

2) the need for the education of our children to be good stewards and the need for models of good discipleship and stewardship;

3) the connection between stewardship and social justice and the need for a converted heart.

Joseph Cardinal Tomko and Archbishop Paul Josef Courdes also spoke at the conference. Both pointed out that evangelization and stewardship are the work of all baptized Christians. Because all Catholics belong to a church where 99 percent of its members are the laity, there is a universal need to call everyone to the ministries of evangelization and stewardship.

Joseph Cardinal Tomko, prefect of the Congregation on the Evangelization for all People, in ending his excellent talk on "Stewardship: a Way of Evangelization" said that:

> evangelization is the action of bringing the Gospel, the message of Jesus Christ, to all people. Through proper stewardship of our time, talent, and treasure, each individual can participate actively and fruitfully in the work of evangelization. And similarly, good stewardship can be seen as a proper way of evangelization.
>
> (NCSC *Resource,* 1999)

Dr. Elinor Ford, who spoke on "The Importance of Stewardship to Children in the Universal Church," and Archbishop Fernando Capalla of DAVAO in the Philippines discussed the need for good models and mentors for the twenty-first century. Jesus taught by example and Mary, Mother of Jesus, has for two thousand years been proclaimed as a model of stewardship. Children learn by example. They want us to "walk the talk."

When our children participate in stewardship, they are learning by doing.

Dr. Ford spoke of children this way:

> Before we can talk or teach anything about faith, we must walk with them, so that they can at first see and feel us live faith. Before we can present our young people . . . with the why and how of stewardship, we must first present them with tried manual of our lives. From these, they must see and feel our passion for God, for living God's life, and for carrying God's word to the home, to the parish, and to the marketplace.
>
> (NCSC *Resource,* 1999)

I believe our children are not our future, but our present. They bring life and joy to our worship and our parish life. The need for models and mentors is not limited to young children for we are all the children of God, a loving and caring Father. Therefore, we all—laity and pastors—need models and mentors of stewardship as a way of life and examples of men and women who are living and who have lived their faith. In the Catholic faith, our models have historically come from our saints, but we need to acknowledge our modern-day "saints," as well . . . those baptized Christians who, according to St. Paul, are living in faith.

In his address entitled "Spirituality and Formation in Stewardship," Archbishop Capalla spoke to the need of modeling and mentoring. He cites the example of Richardo J. Cardinal Vidal, Archbishop of Cebu, "who used to have his newly ordained priests live with him for a period of time. Not only can this promote bonds of brotherhood between bishops and priests, it can also serve as a period of pastoral and stewardship formation (NCSC *Resource,* 1997).

In his address entitled "Stewardship: a Converted Heart and Social Justice," Archbishop Marcel Gervais of Ottawa spoke about his change from looking at stewardship as merely speaking about money to regarding it as the stewardship of our time, talent, and treasure:

> I saw in myself a change of heart and made myself speak of the responsibility of all the faithful to move from being

consumers of the sacraments to being participants in the life
of the Church. To give of oneself and one's time, to share
one's skills and abilities, to share one's possessions, according to need, that is the way of the future for us all.

He spoke of global solidarity in the practice of stewardship
and stressed that when one's heart is converted to stewardship,
social justice changes from a second offering at Mass to seeing
the mission of the Gospel as literally changing the world in the
name of a compassionate Christ. We believe that Christ, working through the Catholic Church, is bringing the Kingdom of
God to the world:

> We stewards of the Kingdom have the happy job of pro-
> claiming the vision of the earth without hunger, a world of
> solidarity and harmony between nations. We have the happy
> task of bringing hundreds and millions on board to create a
> climate for change. We have the exciting opportunity to show
> our people a world that is ready for challenge. We want to
> make real our prayer that the Father's Kingdom come "on
> earth" now, as it is in Heaven.
>
> (NCSC *Resource,* 1999)

At the National Catholic Stewardship Conference in Minneapolis in September 1999, the NCSC voted to change its
name to the International Catholic Stewardship Council. This
title better reflects its international membership and will better
serve its purpose in the Catholic Church.

2

How to Construct Sixty-Second Stewardship Sermons

Experience has led me to believe that a sixty-second steward-ship sermon from every pastor or liturgical minister of every church every Sunday either during the service or printed in the bulletin would significantly aid our members to understand what their church is accomplishing through their giving of their time, talent, and treasure. Surely, this would inspire increased giving to fulfill the mission of the church.

Gather together the stewardship committee of your church and at a parish/pastoral council meeting make a list of exactly what the Sunday offering—your members' giving of time, abilities, and money—is accomplishing through your church. Do not limit this list to your own church ministries alone, but also include what the offering accomplishes in the community and the larger church in the name of Jesus Christ. This experience is satisfying for the stewardship committee, the members of the parish/pastoral council, and the clergy, all of whom will feel a sense of accomplishment and well-being when they see clearly exactly what their parish is doing with its ministry.

Keep this list and check off from it each Sunday's accomplish-ments. Then, thank your parish.

Each Sunday I focus on a verse from Scripture or a special day in the church year, such as Palm Sunday, or an event in the life of our church, such as the opening of religious education classes. Turning to the cross references in the back of this book, read the appropriate sermons for inspiration and examples. Memorize one of these or construct your own. Suppose, for example, the weekly Scripture is Heb 13:16:

> Do not neglect to do good and to share what you have; God
> is pleased by sacrifices of that kind.

In the cross references, you will find that Heb 13:16 is covered in G-11 and CY-24: Read the Sermons; copy one and type it out or revise it in your own words. Then share it at the Preparation of the Gifts or print it in the Sunday leaflet and bulletin.

Another example: If next Sunday is Palm Sunday, you will find it listed in the sermons for the Church Year and cross-referenced under Scripture (CY-14 & CY-15). Memorize one of these sermons or write one of our own perhaps using Matt 21:1-11; Mark 11:1-11; Luke 19:29-46; or John 12:12-16.

You might also use an event in the life of Christ or an event in the life of your own parish. By using these sixty-second sermons you will be thanking your people for giving their time, abilities, and money to enable your parish to accomplish its mission—and to make it possible to worship and serve in the name of Jesus.

3

Sixty-Second Stewardship Sermons

Preparation of the Gifts—Church Year

CY-1

First Sunday of Advent

Matt 24:37-44   Mark 13:33-37   Luke 21:25-28; 34-36

For Catholics, this Sunday marks the beginning of our church year. It is a season of expectation and preparation for the birth of Jesus Christ.

———

Today is the first Sunday of Advent—the New Year. It is a time we prepare our hearts and souls for the coming birth of Christ. It is a time of expectation, of watchfulness, and a time of self-examination. We examine our stewardship of time, talent, and treasure and consider how we are using all three for the proclaiming of God's kingdom. Thank you for your offering today. It will go toward building God's kingdom.

———

Happy New Year! Today we begin a new year at [insert name of church]. We are preparing with expectation for the birth of

Jesus on December 25. We are told by the world around us to buy, buy, buy to show our love for our loved ones. We are told by the world to use money we do not have, to buy things we do not need, to impress people we do not even like. Our gifts given at church each week show our appreciation for God's love for us. It is our gift, given to God weekly. Thank you for your stewardship that enables us to proclaim the Son of God, Jesus!

CY-2

December 8
Solemnity of the Immaculate Conception

An essential quality of Stewardship is generosity. The celebration of the Immaculate Conception is a remembrance of the beginning of God's ultimate act of generosity. His Son, Christ Jesus, second person of the Trinity, the God-man who is the Redeemer of the World. He is the Christ who has died, the Christ who has risen, and the Christ who will come again.

God is the ultimate planner and he does nothing without exceeding preparation. The creation of man and the redemption of man are the greatest examples. God created the Garden of Perfection, but Adam and Eve desecrated that place of divine beauty. In the fullness of time, God created another garden, a garden so pure that He would send his own Son into it—this new Garden's name was Mary. This special purity of hers we call the Immaculate Conception.

At the first moment of her conception, Mary was in virtue of the anticipated merits of the Redemption, preserved free from the stain of Adam and Eve that we call Original Sin.

There had to be some creature like Mary, or God would find no person in whom he could take his human origin. Would the All-Perfect God take his human body from one who was not humanly perfect? There had to be an infinite separation between God and sin. Therefore, the Immaculate Conception was essential to the Word becoming flesh.

Truly, having raised one woman by preserving her from sin, God gave great hope to our weak and neurotic humankind. Believe that one simple prayer to the Mother of God can lead a person who is not good to become better. Believe that one simple prayer to her, because she is without sin, can make us less sinful.

One last thought. We are all in love with an ideal love. That ideal love is beyond human or creature-love. Now, this ideal love, God has for all eternity—the woman He and we call "Mother." She will always lead us to Christ. She is and always will be the "Gate of Heaven." May the Immaculate Mother of God and of the Church give us hope! Mary, conceived without sin, pray for us who have recourse to you!

Matthew R. Paratore
Secretary General,
*   International Catholic Stewardship Council, Inc.*
Washington, D.C.

CY-3

Nota para el Sermón
Para el día de la Inmaculada Concepción

Una característica esencial de la administración de los bienes de Dios es la generosidad. La celebración de la Inmaculada Concepción sirve para recordarnos del comienzo del mayor acto generoso de Dios: Su Hijo, Jesucristo, segunda persona de la Trinidad, el Dios-Hombre que es el Redentor del Mundo. Él es el Cristo que murió, el Cristo que resucitó, y el Cristo que nuevamente volverá.

Dios es el mejor planificador. Él no hace nada sin prepararse al máximo. La creación y la redención del hombre son los mayores ejemplos. Dios creó el Jardín de la Perfección, pero Adán y Eva mancillarón ese lugar de tanta belleza Divina. A través del tiempo, Dios creó otro jardín, un jardín tan puro que Él enviaría allí a Su propio Hijo. El nombre de ese nuevo jardín es María. Su pureza especial la llamámos la Inmaculada Concepcíon.

María fue, en el mismo instante de la concepción, por razón de los beneficios anticipados de la Redención, libre de la "mancha" de Adán y Eva, esa que llamámos Pecado Original.

Tenía que haber una criatura como María, o Dios no encontraría en quien asumir Su condición humana. ¿Iba acaso Dios, todo perfecto, a tomar su cuerpo humano de alguien que no fuera humanamente perfecta? Tenía que haber una separación infiníta entre Dios y el pecado. Por lo tanto, la Inmaculada Concepción fue esencial en la conversión de la Palabra en carne.

En verdad, al haber criado a una mujer sin pecado, y al haber ella acceptado esa ofrenda durante la Anunciación. Dios dio gran esperanza a nuestra débil y neurótica humanidad. Es de creer que una simple oración a la Madre de Dios puede hacer que una persona buena se convierta en alguien mejor. Es de que una simple oración a ella, porque no tiene pecado, puede hacernos menos pecadores.

Por último, todos estámos enamorados con un amor ideal. Ese amor ideal va más alla del amor humano o de cualquier otra criatura. Ese amor ideal Dios lo ha tenido durante toda la eternidad—la Mujer que Él y nosotros llamámos "Madre." Ella siempre nos llevará a Cristo. Ella es y siempre será la "Puerta del Cielo."

Qué la Inmaculada Madre de Dios y de la Iglesia nos llene de esperanza. María, concebida sin pecado, ruega, por nosotros los que venimos a ti!

> *Mateo del Rosario Paratore*
> *Secretario General, Consilio Internacional Católico*
> *de la Administración de los Bienes de Dios*

CY-4

December 8

Solemnity of the Immaculate Conception

Mary Immaculate is the enemy of Satan and victorious over him from the first Annunciation of the Resurrection. She will enlighten, protect, and sustain us all during our earthly battle until we reach our eternal reward.

Mary Immaculate! We should have great consolation thinking about her, who has a God-willed enmity against Satan: "I will put enmity between you and the woman" (Gen 3:15). She is immaculate because she was never stained by original sin or by actual sin, that is, she never gave in to Satan. She is always Virgin, because she always belongs to God, in body as well as soul, and from her, the Word received his body.

Mary declared herself the servant of the Lord, and she became the Mother of God. Mary, our Mother, the Mother of the Church, the Mediatrix of all graces, constantly shows us her dynamic works by the will of Christ, who chose to associate his Mother in his Work of the sanctification of souls.

Mary Immaculate shows us her decisive opposition to all of Satan's works, because they are directed against God's plan for us, and it is to this end that Satan persecutes us, tempts us in every possible way, and, not satisfied to be the root of all evil, sin, pain, and death, tries to drag us with him to eternal damnation and desolation.

On this Solemnity of the Immaculate Conception, we pray for the Church and, in particular, for our bishops and all in sacred orders who are obligated to take on the responsibility of all who suffer because of the devil. May they ever respond to the needs of souls crying to heaven and do so in accordance with the laws and traditions of the Church.

Let us realize the importance of the Marian dogma that Mary ever Virgin, in opposition to Satan, is an instrument of the divine plan.

Mary, conceived without sin, pray for us who have recourse to you!

> *Matthew R. Paratore*
> *Secretary General,*
> *International Catholic Stewardship Council, Inc.*
> *Washington, D.C.*

CY-5

Sermón Número Dos
Para el 8 de diciembre,
día de la Inmaculada Concepción

María Inmaculada es enemiga de Satanás y victoriosa contra él desde primer anuncio de la Resurrección. Ella nos iluminará, protegerá y sostendrá durante nuestra batalla terrenal hasta que alcancémos nuestra recompensa eterna.

¡María Inmaculada! Sentímos gran consuelo al pensar en ella, a quien Dios le hace sentir enemistad contra Satanás: "Hare que tu y la mujer sean enemigas . . ." (Gen 3:15).

Ella es inmaculada porque nunca fue mancillada con el pecado común; es decir que ella nunca se entregó a Satanás. Siempre fue Virgen porque siempre le perteneció a Dios, tanto en cuerpo como en alma, y a través de ella la Palabra recibió Su Cuerpo.

María se declaró la servidora del Señor y se convirtió en la Madre de Dios. María, nuestra Madre, la Madre de la Iglesia, la Mediadora de todas las gracias, constantemente nos demuestra sus trabajos dinámicos por la voluntad de Cristo, quien eligió asociar a su madre con su trabajo de la santificación de las almas.

María Inmaculada nos demuestra su oposición decisiva a todo lo que Satanás hace porque este lo hace contra el plan de Dios para nosotros. Es por eso que Satanás nos persigue, nos tenta de todas las maneras posibles y, no satisfecho de ser la raíz de toda maldad, pecado, dolor y muerte, trata de arrastrarnos con él a la maldición y desolación eternas.

En este día de la Inmaculada Concepción, rogámos por la Iglesia, y en particular por nuestros obispos y todas las ordenes sagradas, quiénes están obligados a ser responsables por aquellos que sufren por causa del diablo. Qué siempre respondan a las necesidades de las almas que claman al cielo y qué lo hagan de acuerdo a las leyes y tradiciones de la Iglesia.

Tomémos cuenta de la importancia del dogma de María; que María, siempre Virgen, opuesta a Satanás, es un instrumento del plan divino.

María, concebida sin pecado, ¡ruega para nostros los que venimos a ti!

Mateo del Rosario Paratore
Secretario General, Consilio Internacional Católico
de la Administración de los Bienes de Dios

CY-6

Sunday within the Octave of Christmas
Holy Family
Presentation of Jesus

Luke 2:22-40

The Feast of the Presentation of Jesus in the Temple had profound spiritual implications for his mother, Mary. Following the prescriptions of the Law, Mary and Joseph offered the child to the Heavenly Father with the usual symbolic sacrifice. Mary understood that with that offering she was also making a total offering of herself to carry out her role in accord with God's will. If she had any doubts that her life would entail severe suffering, they were not dissipated by the prophet Simeon who held the Savior of the world in his arms and, looking at her, predicted that a sword would pierce her soul as well. How painful that sword was to be would only be revealed years later.

Every time we participate in the Eucharist, we too are making a presentation. We too are asked to offer the sacrifice of ourselves; we too accept the will of the heavenly Father, although its full implications are still hidden from our eyes. Holy Mary, give us the courage to accept our future as you did yours when you presented the child in the Temple. Give us the insight to know that whatever God sends us will be for our salvation and ultimate happiness.

Most Rev. James Keleher
Archbishop of Kansas City in Kansas

CY-7

The Epiphany of the Lord
The Coming of the Wise Men

Matt 2:1-12

Today, we remember the coming of the Wise Men to the baby Jesus in Bethlehem. They brought with them their gifts of gold, frankincense, and myrrh. This morning, we brought with us our parish envelope as our gift to the Christ Child, to pay him homage. We do this each time we gather together. We, like the Wise Men, bring our gifts to honor our Lord and Savior. Thank you for your generous gifts. You are enabling [insert name of church] to tell the story.

––––––––

Wise men and wise women still seek him! The Wise Men journeyed from the East to find the Christ Child, Jesus. We have traveled to [insert name of church] this morning seeking Jesus, and we have brought our gifts that represent gold, frankincense, and myrrh. Our offering this morning is ourselves—our time, talent, and treasure. By our gifts, we are making Jesus known throughout our world.

CY-8

The Baptism of the Lord

Matt 3:13-17   Mark 1:7-11   Luke 3:15-16; 21-22

Today we remember the baptism of Jesus Christ in the river Jordan, by John the Baptist. In all of the accounts from Matthew, Mark and Luke, God proclaims from heaven words such as: "This is my beloved Son; with whom I am well pleased." This affirmation begins the ministry of Jesus. In our own baptism we begin our ministry, our stewardship of time, talent, and treasure. I give thanks for your stewardship-ministry at [insert name of church].

––––––––

The baptism of Jesus by John at the river Jordan begins Christ's ministry. I pray that each of us in our own ministry and stewardship hears the words of God: "You are my beloved son; with you I am well pleased." I thank our Father for your faithful stewardship of time, talent, and treasure. You are enabling us "to worship and serve in Jesus' name."

CY-9

Dr. Martin Luther King's Birthday

1 Cor 12:4-12

It was to build up the Church, as St. Paul says, that God handed over these gifts to his children in order to unite them with the Lord and each other. Those who thought they had no gifts envied those who had; those with only one gift envied those with several. In correcting the Corinthian community, Paul assures them that all are being led by the spirit and there is no room for jealousy as we share the gifts of time, talent, and treasure. Dr. King used his God-given gifts to help rebuild our society and never shied away from giving his time, talent, and treasure. May we generously give of our gifts, as well, for the building up of the kingdom of God in our midst.

Rev. James V. Matthews
St. Benedict Church
Oakland, California

CY-10

Ash Wednesday

Joel 2:12-18   Matt 6:1-6; 16-18

In the Catholic tradition Ash Wednesday is the first day of Lent. Ashes are made available to those who choose to receive them.

———

Jesus tells us that when we give, it should be done in secret. That is one reason for our church envelopes—what you give should be known only to God. God cares about what we do. Today we have received ashes symbolizing our mortality and penitence. "Remember that you are dust, and to dust you shall return." Remember, too, as the Gospel tells us, "Turn from sin and believe in the Good News!" There is an the old Jewish saying: "There are no pockets in the shroud!"

———

Today we remember our mortality and penitence; it is a time for self examination. Each time we make our gifts at the offering, we are affirming a new way of godly life. I thank you for our repentance and faith this night (day).

CY-11

First Sunday of Lent

Matt 4:1-11   Mark 1:12-15   Luke 4:1-13

Today, Jesus is tempted. We are often tempted not to live up to our highest potential as children of God. Like Jesus, our temptations may not be so much to do evil as to choose some lesser good. Often we do this with our giving. We choose to be less giving than we know we could be, less generous than we think we should be. Subtly, the devil tempts us to think that our gift is sufficient. Lent is a time for reminding us that the Lord calls us to the highest form of discipleship and the most challenging aspects of giving. Lent calls us to be more generous and to take hold of life to its fullest.

The Rt. Rev. Robert Ihloff
Episcopal Bishop of Maryland
Baltimore

For forty days, Jesus took stock of his life—who he was and what he wanted to accomplish. We call this forty-day period Lent. Christians are called in Lent to a special period of taking stock, of setting priorities, of rethinking what it means to be a steward of God's gift. May this holy season be a time for you to contemplate anew the many blessings of God and to respond to God by a generous giving of your very selves. Generous giving always brings rewards, as our Lord found out. And while generous giving does not protect us from the difficulties and vagaries of life, it does assure us of a deeper life. As surely as Lent ends with Easter, so a life of giving ends with a greater sense of satisfaction and greater joy.

The Rt. Rev. Robert Ihloff
Episcopal Bishop of Maryland
Baltimore

CY-12

Second Sunday of Lent
Transfiguration

Matt 17:1-9   Mark 9:2-10   Luke 9:28-36

When Jesus goes to the mountain with Peter, James, and John, he is transfigured. We celebrate this transfiguration on August 6 and on the Second Sunday of Lent.

Today we remember the Transfiguration. Jesus is transfigured by God, and God speaks: "This is my beloved Son. Listen to him" (Mark 9:7). We are called to listen to Jesus, and by his teaching we live our lives as children of God. Jesus lived his life intimately with the disciples. We too are called upon, as part of our stewardship, to live our lives with love and compassion with those whom God has given us. Your generous offerings help us to live and proclaim God's love at [insert name of church].

The Transfiguration is one of the great feasts of the Christian year. God proclaims to Jesus and to the disciples: "This is my chosen Son; listen to him" (Luke 9:35). Jesus is affirmed by God. Each Sunday, we at [insert name of church] are affirmed as beloved children of God. Your generous gifts of time, talent, and treasure make this affirmation possible. Thank you.

CY-13

The Annunciation of Our Lord
March 25

Luke 1:38

The impressive and attractive Basilica of the Annunciation sits in the middle of the modern city of Nazareth. It is a two-tiered church with a lower and upper floor. Mass can be celebrated simultaneously in both places. The lower church contains an open chapel, sunk deeper than the entry floor. One side of this chapel has an opening into the cave or grotto believed to be the location of the Annunciation event we find in Luke 1:26-38.

When I visited the basilica on a recent pilgrimage to the Holy Land, I found myself drawn immediately into a deep mood of prayer and adoration. Obviously, the basilica serves as a touching reminder of the Annunciation's singular role in the story of our redemption. Furthermore, the basilica exudes a deep peace and is, unmistakably, a place of faith, whether for Christians from Nazareth itself or for visitors and pilgrims from elsewhere.

I would dare to suggest the reason for this atmosphere of faith points to the fact that this holy ground speaks of a singular self-giving that initiated the life of Jesus of Nazareth, our Savior and Lord.

Two thousand years ago, the young woman named Mary responded as the perfect steward to an extraordinary call and invitation. She first wrestled with the complexities of the message given to her by the Angel Gabriel and while uncertain of all it implied for her own future, ultimately said, simply and directly: "Behold, I am the handmaid of the Lord. May it be done to me according to your word" (Luke 1:38).

Cardinal Newman, in a sermon entitled "The Reverence Due to Her," spoke these words: "God was taking upon Him her flesh, and humbling himself to be called her offspring; such is a deep mystery." It is also our mystery as well.

As we wrestle with the complexities of our call and invitation to be good stewards, we can learn from the modeling of Stewardship provided by Mary of Nazareth. Without knowing for certain where a fully generous sharing of our time, treasure, and talent will lead us in the future, we say in trust, "Here I am, the servant of the Lord, let it be done with me according to your word."

Most Rev. Sylvester D. Ryan
Bishop of Monterey

CY-14

Palm Sunday of the Lord's Passion
Liturgy of the Palms

Matt 21:1-11   Mark 11:1-10   Luke 19:28-40   John 12:12-16

Today, we remember Jesus' entrance into Jerusalem. He comes from the village of Bethany riding on a donkey and is proclaimed the Messiah: "Hosanna to the Son of David! Blessed is he who comes in the name of the Lord; Hosanna in the highest!" As part of his stewardship, a poor villager has provided the donkey for Jesus to ride. In such a small, yet significant way, we, too, provide for the ministry of Christ. May we in our own stewardship be as faithful as this unnamed villager.

––––––––––

Today, we have re-enacted the coming of Jesus into Jerusalem. We have blessed the palms and held them as we proclaimed Jesus as LORD! Those in Jerusalem used the palms to wave and cover the road. Then, those who honored Jesus used palms; today, we honor him in our own way as we proclaim him our Lord and Savior. Our gifts, generously given this day, enable [insert name of church] to proclaim this Holy Week the wonderful story of God's redemption for humankind.

CY-15

Palm Sunday of the Lord's Passion

Today is a day of jarring contrast. We have welcomed Jesus into Jerusalem, but we have also participated in the story of his crucifixion. In a short period of time those who have sung his praises turn against Jesus and cry out, "Crucify him!" This contrast says something sobering about human nature. It is easy to give lip service or even to become excited about something new. When we discover that it may cost us, especially if that cost is personal or dear, it may be much more difficult to keep our enthusiasm. Serving God as a steward requires that we really give of ourselves for the long term. God calls us to respond with more than lip service. True discipleship manifests itself in giving our all—giving of our time, our talents, and our treasure—that the work of God can be done and the blessings we have can be shared.

The Rt. Rev. Robert Ihloff
Episcopal Bishop of Maryland
Baltimore

––––––––––

We welcome Jesus this day as our Lord and Savior. It is easy to be enthusiastic, even to be carried away briefly with that enthusiasm. It is much harder to sustain enthusiasm, because that means giving of ourselves. Is it any wonder that many who welcomed Jesus in Jerusalem fell away in their enthusiasm or even turned against him? The Lord gave his all. In so doing, he invites us to be more generous, to give of our very selves that the ministry of love and reconciliation may spread throughout the world. At the beginning of this holiest week, let us pledge ourselves to be more generous, to be more giving. And let us pray that our enthusiasm may not wane, but remain strong for the glory of God and the welfare of our community.

> *The Rt. Rev. Robert Ihloff*
> *Episcopal Bishop of Maryland*
> *Baltimore*

CY-16

Holy Thursday

1 Cor 11:23-26   John 13:1-15

Today, we remember the Institution of the Eucharist, Paul's First letter to the Corinthians, and in John, the Great Commandment and the Washing of the Feet.

———

Tonight, we remember the time Jesus instituted the Eucharist and shared with his disciples the passion meal in a new way that would change our world forever. Tonight, when the bread and wine are presented, think of that first time. Jesus will be betrayed and fastened to the cross tomorrow. At this moment we say, "Thank you." I say thank you for all the wonderful gifts, including the gift of yourselves to God at God's altar tonight and at every Eucharist.

———

In the Gospel of John, Jesus demonstrates what it means to love one another by washing the feet of his disciples. Jesus taught his stewardship by example. Tomorrow, he will give his life for us, a sacrifice, so that we will have no doubt just how much he and God love us. Tonight, our offerings of humility and service are given in response to his love for us. I thank you for being here tonight, as we share together this time with Jesus.

CY-17

Good Friday of the Lord's Passion

John 18:1-19, 42

The Catholic Church sends its Good Friday offering to the Holy Land Shrines in Jerusalem for the work of Jesus Christ in that part of the world. Like Paul, we remember our Christians living and praying in Jerusalem. (Suggestion: This sermon could be printed in the bulletin.)

––––––––

Today we remember the ultimate sacrifice of Jesus on the cross. As an act of his ultimate stewardship, he gave all that he had—gave his very life for us, to remove any doubts we might have about how much we are loved by God. The offering we give today is for the first church founded in Jerusalem. I have seen the work being done in the Holy Land by this church, even under persecution, and how it is witnessing to the resurrection of Jesus Christ in a hostile world. I ask you to be generous.

––––––––

Today is Good Friday. It is called "good" because on this day Christ died for us that we would know eternal life. Tonight, our Good Friday offering goes to the first church founded in Jerusalem as a witness to our faith. It is part of our stewardship of money here at [insert the name of the church]. I have seen the godly work this church in Jerusalem is doing under extremely hostile and difficult conditions. I thank you for your generous response.

CY-18

Easter Sunday

John 20:1-9

Today, we gather to celebrate the resurrection of Jesus Christ. We have sung wonderful hymns that speak of our praise, adoration, and joy! But, in reality, every Sunday in the Christian Church is an Easter Sunday because we remember Christ's resurrection each week. I thank you for your generous weekly offerings, your stewardship of your time, your talent, and your treasure. They make it possible for [insert name of the church] to be able to preach the Easter message every day.

———

It is a wonderful day for the church of Jesus Christ as the faithful members of his congregation gather to worship him on the day of his resurrection. Throughout the world, the message of his triumph over death and Good Friday is being told. I am thankful that God has brought us together at [insert name of church] to rejoice and praise Jesus and to share in his Holy Eucharist. We offer ourselves this morning—our time, our talent, and our treasure. By telling of the story, Jesus will be made known. Thank you!

CY-19

Pentecost Sunday

Acts 2:1-11

We celebrate Pentecost as part of the three days that changed our lives forever—Christmas, Easter, and Pentecost. At our church, we request that all parishioners wear something red to remind us of the Holy Spirit. We have a special chasuble made by the Altar Guild from a bed sheet and laid on a table. Each person who comes in is asked to write a message on it to God and sign it with

*red ink for me to wear during the service. On this day, I literally
"wear the church," and this symbolizes that the church is not a
building, but the gathered people of God. At our hospitality hour,
we have a huge sheet cake celebrating the birthday of the church.
Normally, our church is overflowing on this day.*

————

Thank you for being here with the family of [insert name of
church] to celebrate Pentecost today. It is wonderful to see a
sea of red, as we acknowledge that Holy Spirit who inspires our
worship and our faith, and gives us the power, week by week,
to proclaim the kingdom of God. I wear this chasuble, signed
by all of you, to symbolize that we are all the Church—it is not
a building, but the people of God gathered together today. Thank
you for your faithful stewardship of time, talent, and treasure
that enables us to be the church.

————

Today is a day in the life of our church equal to Christmas
and Easter. The first Pentecost, when the Holy Spirit came upon
the disciples, three thousand were baptized by the Holy Spirit.
Today is the church's birthday, and for children of all ages, we
will have a huge birthday cake at our hospitality hour. When
you go to a birthday party, you always bring a gift. Today we
bring our gifts to the church to celebrate its birth. Thank you
for your generous offering this morning. By your gifts, we are
building the church.

CY-20

Twenty-Fourth Sunday in Ordinary Time

A Stewardship Reflection on the Parable of the Prodigal Son

Luke 12:1-32

The story of the prodigal son is so familiar that we almost do not hear it any more. A younger son asks his father for his share of the estate (never mind that dad is not through with it yet!) and goes out and wastes it all wantonly on wine, women, and song. Then "he comes to his senses" and comes home, looking for a dry place to sleep and some leftovers to eat. He is astonished to find that the father he has let down so completely still loves him, giving him a hero's welcome he certainly does not deserve. Usually, the homily preached when this parable is read is all about forgiveness, and rightly so. The two parables immediately before the one about the prodigal son—the shepherd who leaves the ninety-nine sheep who are safe and secure to go after the lost one and the woman who sweeps her house diligently to find the lost coin—are certainly about caring enough to drop everything to search for what is lost and then rejoicing when it is found.

But the story of the prodigal son has some even more profound implications. It is about a love that is all-giving as well as forgiving. It is about a father who holds nothing back, who gives without stinting, and who loves, even when the gifts are squandered and unacknowledged. We almost always focus on the younger son, the prodigal, but the older son, who shows up in the last few paragraphs, is an integral part of the story, too. And, although at first glance the two boys seem very different, one a reckless spendthrift and the other steady and responsible, if you look closely, they really are very much the same. The younger son felt "entitled" to "his share" of the family fortune and was not shy about asking for it and spending it on his pleasure. The other son was equally grasping. He saw all that remained of the estate as his by right and begrudged what the father spent for the prodigal's homecoming. Both were equally self-absorbed. The younger son was self-centered and engaged in self-destructive behavior, thinking of others only when he had lost everything and could no longer satisfy his needs. The older son was self-centered and self-righteous, which may have been the point of the story, because, remember, Jesus told the story in response to smug, self-satisfied Pharisees who were criticizing him for consorting with sinners. Both sons were heedless takers, who felt entitled to their father's fortune. Only the father was a giver, and he gave generously, selflessly, patiently, unconditionally—waiting for the lost one to come home and forgiving him as well as soothing the mean-spirited elder son and reassuring him of his father's love.

How like these boys we often are! We believe that what we have, we have by right and we forget that all of it is a gift. How often we forget that all we have and all we are comes from God. He gives it unconditionally and he loves us, whether we use our gifts wisely or squander them away thoughtlessly. And he waits patiently, like the father in the parable, for us to look up from our self-absorption and see that all we have is his! When we begin to see that, we can begin to be grateful. And that gratitude takes us beyond ourselves to others, moves us from selfishness to sharing. When we become grateful recipients of the gifts of God, instead of heedless takers who feel entitled, we begin to want to be givers ourselves.

> *Sharon Hueckel*
> *Director of Pastoral Office for Development*
> *Diocese of Lafayette in Indiana*

CY-21

Thirty-Third Sunday in Ordinary Time
"It's Time!"

Mark 13:32

As faithful stewards, we are accountable for how we use our gifts: TREASURE and how our parish and community depend upon our generosity; TALENT and how we struggle to help our parish bring Jesus' healing touch to our world; and TIME and how our stewardship is exercised by the time we give it. If Jesus came to us today and asked each of us for an accounting of what we have done with our gifts, what would we tell him? You know that Jesus will ask us how we used our lives, with how much love we reached out to others, with what diligence we worked for the building up of his kingdom of love, justice, and peace. There are many ways to place your time, talent, and treasure. Your parish and community have many needs which only you can fulfill. You have only to step forward, because: "It is time!"

Rev. James V. Matthews
St. Benedict Church
Oakland, California

CY-22

The Assumption of the Blessed Virgin Mary

Luke 1:39-56

The Feast of the Assumption of Mary on August 15 celebrates Mary's passage to heaven—body and soul.

The biblical concept of "assumption" dates back to the Old Testament where it appears that those who have seen God or who have received revelations of him are members of a select group that need to be "taken" to heaven when they die.

Although we have observed this feast in various ways since the fifth century, the New Testament does not affirm this happening. It appears to have grown from the Church's life of prayer, biblical reflection, and sacrament. In the eighth century, the feast became known as the Assumption and was universally observed in the West. Indeed, it was not until 1950 that Pope Pius XII defined her assumption as being "taken up"—body and soul.

As we celebrate the Assumption, we listen to the Magnificat as Mary praises God and acknowledges his greatness and the wonderful things he has done for her. She recognizes that many will benefit as she allows God to work through her. So, too, will others benefit as we open ourselves to the grace of God, accepting his favor and passing it on as good stewards of his many blessings.

Catherine Coghlan
Office of Stewardship and Development
Archdiocese of Kansas City in Kansas

CY-23

The Assumption of the Blessed Virgin Mary

Luke 1:39-56

The Church celebrates the feast of the Assumption of Mary on August 15. It directs our attention to how Mary passed from this earth and what the implications are for us as we honor her.

In the sixth century the feast focused on the "Dormition of Mary" or the "falling asleep" of Mary. Our understanding now is that Mary is not "asleep" but rather awake. When we pray to her with our prayers of intercession, we picture someone who is responsive and listening.

In Luke 1:39-56 we read about Mary's visit to Elizabeth and Mary's response (the Magnificat) to Elizabeth's greeting. As Elizabeth honors Mary for trusting God, we are reminded that all the honor we give to Mary is actually praise to God for all the marvelous things God has done in and through Mary.

As we listen or read Luke's Gospel, we rejoice and give thanks and praise to God for how he works in each and every one of our lives everyday. It is through his grace that we are able to accept his blessings, develop and share them, and then return them as gifts to the Father. Thus is the life of a steward.

Catherine Coghlan
Office of Stewardship and Development
Archdiocese of Kansas City in Kansas

CY-24

Last Sunday in Ordinary Time
Christ the King

Matt 25:31-46

The Least of These

Jesus' story of the Last Judgment tells us of our duty and responsibilities to "these least brothers of mine." Truly, it is *most* of God's children and our brethren, not the *least* of them, who are hungry, naked, thirsty, sick, and imprisoned. They are the majority of mankind, representing somewhere between one-half and two-thirds of *God's* children. "The least of these" are being consumed with the struggle for mere survival.

The word *least* might refer to our attitudes and understanding of the needs of the hungry and naked peoples of this world, who are nearby as well as far off. What does Jesus have to say about our position in life among the "haves" when there are so many "have-nots"? What are our attitudes about the desperate in this world? Can we as Christians close our hearts to them? Surely, we cannot.

Our part in the war against hunger and poverty begins and ends with our Christian commitment or lack of the same. We are called upon to be good stewards of God's many gifts. We are to conserve, protect, and husband the resources of his world as a beginning, but our Christian responsibility calls out to us:

> Do not neglect to do good and to share what you have; God is pleased by sacrifices of that kind (Heb 13:16).

We who are called upon to minister to all peoples dare not be content and ignore "the least of these."

Canon W. David Crockett
Episcopal Diocese of Western Massachusetts
Springfield

CY-25

Last Sunday in Ordinary Time
Stewardship Through the Example of Jesus

Matt 25:31-46

For children to recognize the importance of stewardship, it is well to point out that the strongest encounters they have with Jesus Christ are often through other people. Matthew 25 says it succinctly: "Lord, when did we see you hungry or a stranger or naked or ill or in prison and not minister to your needs?" Christ did not simply show an interest towards those in need, somewhat as we might with a letter of introduction: "I shall appreciate your consideration toward . . . ." Rather he said *I* am the one who felt the painful tightening of hunger, I felt the bone-chilling dampness. He said, "Amen, I say to you, what you did not do for the least ones, you did not do for me." A sense of stewardship can allow the young to see compassion and concern in an entirely new light when they are taught stewardship through the example of Jesus.

> Rev. Francis W. Wright, C.S.Sp.
> National Director, Holy Childhood Association
> Washington, D.C.

CY-26

November 2—All Souls

Matt 5:1-12

At the All Souls' service at our church, we remember by name all those who have been buried from the church during the past year. We also mention all of those who have asked to be remembered on a sign-up list in the entryway to the church. In addition, I send a personal letter to the families of all who have been buried, and we invite them to be present as we remember their loved ones by name.

————

Today, we have remembered by name all who have died, and we pray that through God's mercy, our loved ones are now with God in Paradise. We appreciate their past stewardship. By their sharing of their time, talent, and treasure, [insert name of church] stands here, a holy place on a hill. By example, they have taught us what it means to be a loving, caring Christian, committed to doing God's work through this church.

————

This morning, we give thanks for all of those we have re-membered by name, who we pray are now in God's kingdom. We appreciate all that they did throughout their lives to prac-tice good stewardship with their time, talent, and treasure to have made our church the church that it is today. I pray that through our stewardship, we can continue to "worship and serve in Jesus' name."

CY-27

November 2—All Souls

Matt 5:1-12

On this day we remember all those who have come before us in our families, in our parish, and in our community. We are part of an intricate web of relationships with many people. These saints remain among us in our inheritances. In our parish, look around and see what the legacies are in our worship, minis-tries, and physical surroundings. In our personal lives, we are a part of the past in our present circumstances. In the commu-nity, we are surrounded by the programs and institutions of past men and women who contributed and loved sacrificially. Such reflections pose a question: What are *we* doing with what *we* have inherited—to maintain, strengthen, and grow in our parish, personal life, and ministries, in our neighborhood and community? What do we wish to leave for others? To paraphrase a Scouts' slogan: How can we leave our campsite cleaner than we found it?

The Rev. Ronald L. Reed
Pastor, St. James Episcopal Church
Wichita

CY-28

Thanksgiving Eve

At my church we do not have a Thanksgiving Day service. Thanksgiving morning is a difficult time for people to come and worship. Parishioners are traveling to Grandmother's. Family is coming for dinner and everyone is busy cooking. Church members are attending high school football games. Instead, we worship on Thanksgiving Eve. Our twenty-four member men's chorus leads the worship, and we give each family a loaf of freshly baked bread. Tables placed in front of the altar are overflowing with more than one hundred loaves of bread. The whole church smells like a bakery! We ask each family "to reserve" a loaf so that we are sure to have enough.

Tonight, as a symbol of God's love and care for us, we have these tables filled with bread. It smells just like a bakery here. Bread is a gift from God; in the Lord's Prayer, we ask: "Give us this day our daily bread." Tonight, [insert name of church] has a loaf of bread for every family. We have only one request. Please serve it as part of your Thanksgiving dinner. If you are visiting, take it with you. Tell everyone that it is a gift from the church in thanksgiving for all the ministers and members of our church.

The Bread of Life! The food that nourishes us and sustains us. Tonight, we will bless this bread as a sign of God's abundance and generosity. We can smell it—Ummmm—see it, and after the service, you can come forward and feel it. We offer many kinds of bread, representing many nationalities and ethnic origins. We, as Christians, are called to give thanks for all generous gifts. Our offering is a very concrete way we say "Thank you" tonight to God. As pastor, I thank you for your generous spirit and your generous offerings.

Preparation of the Gifts—General

G-1

"Good Giving"

In many churches, clergy exhort their parishioners to "give until it hurts." All we have found is that Catholics have a "very low pain threshold." I hope we will give until it feels *good*. The money we give each week enables [insert name of church] to be a giving, godly force in our community and our world.

————

When we make our special offering this morning for [insert name of church], how do you think God will feel? Will God respond with "That was wonderful! You really shouldn't have done it. Your generosity pleases me. Thank you for your generous gift"? I believe God *does* care. Please be generous.

G-2

Blessings

The German poet Goethe claimed: "Whatever is not used is but a load to bear!" God has gifted us with many blessings: the hours of each day, our individual and corporate talents, some financial resources. When we use these blessings to fulfill the vision and mission of the Gospel, a graced joy sweeps through our lives. However, when we refuse to share our gifts, we are weighed down and life becomes ponderous, if not actually depressing. Let us use well the gifts God has given to us and walk lightly and freely in the way of the Lord.

Most Rev. Robert F. Morneau
Auxiliary Bishop of Green Bay

G-3

Preparation of the Gifts

> Offer praise as your sacrifice to God;
> and fulfill your vows to the Most High (Ps 50:14).

Is the offering in your envelope today a sacrifice of thanksgiving? Is it a true sacrifice for you and your family? Is it given in thanksgiving? We here at [insert name of church] believe that all we have and all our time, talents, and treasure are gifts from a glorious and generous God. Today we are thankfully offering back to God only a part of that which God has given us. I thank you for your faithfulness in your giving.

––––––––

This morning, at this time, we will take up a collection in the offertory baskets. We do this every Mass at [insert name of church]. The psalmist tells us to do this in a spirit of sacrifice and thanksgiving. Sacrifice means that the gift we offer makes a difference in our lives. I thank God for the sacrifices you are making every week in thanksgiving for the way that God has blessed you.

G-4

Presenting Ourselves

> I urge you therefore, brothers, by the mercies of God, to offer
> your bodies as a living sacrifice, holy and pleasing to God,
> your spiritual worship (Rom 12:1).

When we come to church, we offer God three things: our *time;* our *talents*—our abilities to pray, praise, sing, worship; and our *treasure.* God accepts these, because God wants not our gifts, but us as Givers. God wants us. We are the living sacrifice.

––––––––

Did you prepare yourselves today to be a holy and pleasing living sacrifice to God? What kind of sacrifice does God want? How is your stewardship of God's creation sacrificed? Each Mass, we present ourselves at God's Altar—we pray for God's mercy that we and our gifts are acceptable.

G-5

Bringing Gifts

> Give to the LORD the glory due his name!
> Bring gifts, and enter his courts (Ps 96:8)

Each week as you write your check or put your money in your offering envelope, you are making a spiritual act of thanksgiving for all of God's gifts. It is an act of graciousness, of appreciation for God's work throughout our daily lives. Please be generous, for we are returning to God a portion of what God has given us.

———

Each week we gather to praise God through our worship of one God—the Father and Creator; the Son, Redeemer; and the Holy Spirit, Our Sanctifier. We know God when we bring our offerings to the altar. They symbolize our stewardship—the management of our time, talents, and treasure, that which we return to God through God's church to proclaim God's kingdom. Thank you for your generosity.

G-6

Giving First to God

Prov 3:9-10

Becoming a steward in our faith is commitment in its highest form. It is our personal partnership with God: giving our word to support his word. It is saying yes to our faith. And it is a yes that only each one of us can say.

When we say yes to stewardship, we are committing ourselves to the fundamental belief that as we support God, he will support us. Consider this stewardship passage from Proverbs:

> Honor the LORD with your wealth,
>   with the first fruits of all your produce.
> Then will your barns be filled with grain
>   with new wine your vats will overflow.

Although the passage may seem a little out of date, the meaning remains clear: giving first to God is an act of stewardship and an expression of faith.

And so we must ask ourselves: "Is this a belief I hold?" The answer will reflect the depth of our faith.

Chris Deets
Basilica of St. Mary
Minneapolis

G-7

Creator

> Worthy are you, Lord our God,
>   to receive glory and honor and power,
> for you created all things;
>   because of your will they came to be and were created
>   (Rev 4:11).

God is the author of our creation. God created the world and God created us. Often, I hear someone say, "I am a self-made man (or woman)." Such people worship themselves as their own creator. This morning we acknowledge the Lord, our Father—our Creator. We worship not ourselves, but God, who created us. Our stewardship of time, talents, and treasure acknowledges that God created all of us.

This morning, through our worship, we offer God our glory, honor, and power. Our offerings this morning of our time, talent, and treasure are the grateful response of the created, returning to the Creator a gift of God's creation. Through your generous gifts, we here at [insert name of church] proclaim the Creator to the world.

G-8

Offerings

> Give to the LORD the glory due his name!
> Bring gifts, and enter his courts (Ps 96:8).

Your offering envelopes this morning honor our God. Our gifts let God know in a very tangible way how much we honor the name, the person, the courts, and this house—very holy place—made holy by the presence of God this morning. We will give our gifts to God to be blessed and used for God's work in God's church and God's world. I give thanks that you are here this morning to present your offering.

This morning we are bringing our offerings to our Lord, God. We are honoring God's name at [insert name of church]. We are in God's place, the courts where we gather each week to worship God, to know Jesus, to be guided by the Holy Spirit. I give thanks to all who have brought their offerings this morning. Your offerings will enable [insert name of church] to continue to proclaim the Word of God and to be God's church in this holy place.

G-9

Live in Love

> Live in love, as Christ loved us and handed himself over for us as a sacrificial offering to God . . . (Eph 5:2).

Paul tells us to walk in love with Jesus, as Jesus loves us. Jesus died on the cross, because he loves us that much. Our offerings this morning are given in love, in response to the love of Jesus for us. Thank you for your offerings—a living, tangible way of saying, "Jesus, we love you."

_____

Is your offering a sacrifice to God? Jesus gave himself on the cross for us. This morning, we offer ourselves in thanksgiving for Jesus Christ's love for us. It is our sacrifice that the _____ here, [insert the name of your church, parochial school, diocese] can proclaim the love of Jesus Christ.

G-10

Reconciliation

> "Therefore, if you bring your gift to the altar, and there recall that your brother has anything against you, . . . go first and be reconciled with your brother, and then come and offer your gift" (Matt 5:23-24).

This morning's offering relates the gift of money we bring to the altar for others. If you are alienated from your mother or father, your brother or sister, friend, neighbor, or co-worker, make peace with that person today. Be reconciled that your stewardship of time, talent, and treasure will be acceptable to God.

————

This morning, as we present ourselves as an offering to God, if you are alienated from a family member, today may be the day to telephone or visit or write a note to heal that wound and bring about reconciliation. We offer our time, talent, and treasure this morning in thanksgiving for God's reconciling love for each of us.

G-11

Doing Good

> Do not neglect to do good and to share what you have; God is pleased by sacrifices of that kind (Heb 13:16).

We are called upon to do good—"To worship and serve in Jesus' name." We always need to remember that Jesus died for the world and *not* for the church. Your offering this morning will be shared and do good in the world caring for God's children. Thank you.

————

As children, we are born selfish. The first words most children learn after *Mommy* and *Daddy* are *my* and *mine*. As followers of the way of Jesus, we learn to share and to do good. Through our stewardship—the giving of our time, talents, and treasure—we break this guise of selfishness. *Me* and *mine* become *ours*. We work to do God's work in the world. Thank you for your generous gifts this morning to do God's work.

G-12

Joyful Giving

Today will joyfully present our offerings of money to the Lord, but we will offer not just our money. We will present our oblations, the bread and wine, which will be consecrated and then given to us as the body and blood of Christ. The bread and the wine placed on the altar and the money placed in front of it represent us and who we are—our thankfulness to God and our love of Jesus Christ.

———

Our offerings, the money we joyfully give this morning, represent to God our life and labor. Our oblations, the bread and wine, symbolize all of God's gifts to us. Together, they represent our labor, our time and ability—the work for which we are paid. However, God doesn't want just our gifts of money, God wants the givers—us. I thank God you chose to be here at Mass this morning to offer your gifts and yourselves joyfully to God. I thank you for coming to share joyfully with me this Holy Eucharist—Great Thanksgiving!

G-13

Receiving a Hundred-Fold in Return

In our modern, fast-paced lives, it is difficult to find the time or energy to give in the name of our faith, especially since it is difficult to know what we can expect in return!

We work and receive a salary. If we spend time on a hobby, our reward is pleasure. However, when we give to our faith, it is much harder to define what we get back.

It is precisely when we become stewards of our faith that we learn the great paradox of spiritual life. While they are intangible, the rewards from a life of faith are far greater than any we receive from our work or our play. When we donate our time and talents, when we give of our treasure, we sense our faith growing stronger. Our awareness of God's love for us becomes clearer. We feel closer to God than at any other time. And we realize the deep bonds that hold us all together.

We cannot explain it, but we know it is true. When we give what we have to our faith, we receive a hundred-fold in return!

Chris Deets
Basilica of St. Mary
Minneapolis

G-14

Receive, Nurture, Share, Return!

From the Bishops' letter *Disciple's Response,* we find a very simple definition of "stewardship." It goes something like this: Receive God's gifts gratefully, nurture God's gifts responsibly, share God's gifts with charity and justice, and return God's gifts in abundance. For a moment, let us consider these four concepts.

Receive

- Accept God's gift of life on this earth.
- Accept and acknowledge the talents God has given you.
- Accept financial success and what it enables you to accomplish.
- Accept God's forgiveness for our imperfection.
- Accept God's help on a daily basis.

Nurture

- Take care of your health.
- Take care of your environment.
- Take care to use the talents you have been given.
- Take care to organize your time fruitfully.
- Take care to use your finances wisely.

Share

- Give time to your family, your parish, and your community.
- Give your talents for the good of others.
- Give of your worldly possessions to those in need.
- Give financially in proportion to what God has given you.
- Give encouragement so that others will live a life of stewardship.

Return

- Leave this earth a better place.
- Leave a legacy of generosity.
- Leave a spirit of love.
- Leave having used every talent to its fullest.
- Leave NO DOUBT that God came first in your life!

Sandy Ferencz
Director of Stewardship Development
Diocese of Charleston

G-15

Creation

This morning let us think about the stewardship of God's creation. The ecological movement has been raising our consciousness about our endangered earth. God has given us stewardship and management of all creation, and we have littered, polluted, and destroyed it. I believe that Christians need to take over the leadership for a reverence and care of God's creation. We need to capture the sense of the Hebrew Bible that we must care for our children's children by our stewardship of God's earth today.

———

What do you think God thinks about the way we have cared for and used God's creation? Are we treating it lovingly with the tender care it deserves or are we polluting it and destroying it little by little? God has given us stewardship over all creation. At our death, we will be called home to God and I believe we will all be held accountable for the earth we have left for our children's children. I pray that as we practice good stewardship of our time, talent, and treasure, we will practice good stewardship of the earth as well.

G-16

The Good Earth

Today, we thank God for our earth—our planet. We also pray for the good sense to care for it as good stewards. By nature Christians are ecologists. We know God created our earth and saw that it was good. As we practice our personal stewardship, remember: we are accountable to our children and our children's children for the earth we leave them.

————

[Begin with a personalized description of fall in a beautiful local spot in or near your community.]

The leaves are changing colors. The water is crystal blue. What a glorious portrait of God's beauty and creation! I pray that each of us, as part of our stewardship, will conserve this beauty. Our Sunday offering is one way that we thank God for God's creation. Thank you for sharing in this offering of our thanks.

G-17

Reverence for the Earth

Do we have a reverence for the earth as God's creation or do we think of it as a planet to be exploited? Do we use the earth's resources to serve others or only for our own comforts? These questions of stewardship define how we are honoring God. Stewardship is not just the use of our time, talents, and treasure for our parish, but good stewardship is how we care for all of God's world and people. I thank you for being here this morning, as we gather together to thank God for God's creation.

————

We are held accountable for how we treat this planet earth, and how we love, care for, and serve others. It is a "both-and" love for God's creation and for God's children. I thank God that you are here this Sunday as we reverently thank God for God's creation and return to God what has been given to us: our time, our talent, and our treasure to be used for the service of others.

G-18

Human Labor

The offering can be placed in front of the altar in a large basket, thus showing clearly the value we place on the people's gifts.

————

This morning we pray for all human labor to be blessed and for the right use of the riches of creation. Our offering, the money we place in the collection baskets, represents our human labor, our use of our time and our talents, for which we have been paid. This morning our offering placed in front of the altar will be blessed by God for God's work through this church and the parochial schools of this diocese. We pray that these offerings will be used wisely. Thank you for your faithful offerings each week.

————

When the collection is taken this morning, we will place the collection baskets in front of the altar. We say thank you for all of God's blessings upon us. We will then bless this offering and pray that our parish pastoral council will use the money rightly and wisely for the building up of God's kingdom and caring for those suffering from poverty, famine, and disaster. I give thanks for your trust in this parish that we will use the money you give to continue God's work.

G-19

The Camel and the Needle

> "It is easier for a camel to pass through [the] eye of [a] needle than for one who is rich to enter the kingdom of God" (Mark 10:25).

Jesus' whimsical illustration of a camel trying to pass through the eye of a needle certainly does not mean that it is impossible for the wealthy to enter into God's kingdom. It *does* mean that when the piling up of riches becomes an end in itself, rather than a means toward an end, that is debilitating. The rich man's understanding of stewardship is all-important here. Love must be directed toward God and people who can return love, and not toward wealth, which cannot.

Rev. Canon David W. Crockett
Episcopal Diocese of Western Massachusetts
Springfield

G-20

God's Kingdom

> Jesus answered, "My kingdom does not belong to this world" (John 18:36).

Jesus made it amply clear that his kingdom was not of this world. It is neither temporal nor political, but rather is of the spiritual realm. As inheritors of the kingdom of heaven, Christians are in this world, but not of it, and therefore must exercise extraordinary care where we place our allegiances. When we rely on property, possessions, material objects, and wealth, we make "things" our sovereign and place our trust in them rather than in the King of kings. Stewardship helps us to put first things first.

Rev. Canon David W. Crockett
Episcopal Diocese of Western Massachusetts
Springfield

G-21

Last Judgment

Matt 25:31-46

Jesus' story of the Last Judgment tells us of our duty and responsibilities toward the least of our brothers and sisters. Unhappily, the hungry, naked, thirsty, sick, and imprisoned represent the majority of humankind. Our part in the war against hunger and poverty begins with our Christian commitment. You and I are called upon to minister to all peoples and dare not ignore "these least ones."

> *Rev. Canon David W. Crockett*
> *Episcopal Diocese of Western Massachusetts*
> *Springfield*

G-22

Comfort and Challenge

Mic 6:8

God's word is both comforting and challenging. We are comforted in knowing that we are loved and redeemed by the Lord Jesus. We are challenged to respond to that loving redemption by following in the footsteps of the Lord, that life of acting justly, loving tenderly, and walking humbly with our God (Mic 6:8).

We express this life specifically by being good caretakers of God's gifts. We live discipleship by lives of joyful generosity. Thank you for your witness to the Gospel.

> *Most Rev. Robert F. Morneau*
> *Auxiliary Bishop of Green Bay*

G-23

Gratefulness

We need to focus on the many things for which we are grateful. A grateful person is a joyful person and one that understands that everything comes from a loving God. What are you grateful for? Perhaps you are grateful for health or family or a place to live; perhaps it is for your many possessions which are actually more "wants" than "needs." Saying "Thank you" to God, who sent his Son to die for us—what greater gift is there?

Francis "Dutch" Scholtz, Director
Office of Stewardship
Diocese of St. Augustine

G-24

Greed

> Therefore, since we are surrounded by so great a cloud of witnesses, let us rid ourselves of every burden and sin that clings to us and persevere in running the race that lies before us (Heb 12:1).

I want you to close your eyes and imagine that you have suddenly been transported back in time more than fifty years ago, to the year 1946. In your mind's eye, see the persons in the pew in front of you. The man is wearing a uniform, with hash marks on the sleeve. He has just returned from Europe where he served in the infantry. Next to him is his young wife, wearing a red hat with a jaunty feather. The gifts are presented. He reaches into his back pocket to pull out his wallet. Carefully, he removes a folded ten-dollar bill and places it in the offering plate. He is grateful to God for his homecoming to this church where he was baptized twenty-two years before. He bows his head in thanksgiving. Over the many years since, he has put thousands of dollars in that same plate, Sunday by Sunday, as witness to his faith and gratitude. He is here in spirit now, in the pew where he always sat, in his beloved church, and many more are here with him. You are surrounded by a great cloud of unseen witnesses who have given so much. It is now your turn! Make your witness in giving so that others will follow you.

> *The Rev. Roy A. Cole*
> *Specialist for Revitalization*
> *Baltimore*

What is the sin that clings so closely to each and every one of us? Simply put, it is greed. We are a greedy people. We live in a greedy culture that places material goods and access to them as a supreme value. It makes us a greedy people and greed is a sin. In our culture, it is a sin that clings very closely to each one of us, every day, and will continue to do so, unless we decide to do something about it. The remedy for greed is giving. Greedy people need to give to get over their greed and become spiritually healthy. This morning, do something for yourself. Give and give generously until that nervous feeling induced by greed gives away to joy—which is what you feel when you are delivered from a sin that clings so, so closely.

> *The Rev. Roy A. Cole*
> *Specialist for Revitalization*
> *Baltimore*

G-25

Running

> Therefore, since we are surrounded by so great a cloud of witnesses, let us rid ourselves of every burden and sin that clings to us and persevere in running the race that lies before us (Heb 12:1).

I want you to think back to a time when you were a kid and as all kids do, you got into a race. Maybe it was in school, maybe it was with a close friend or your brother or sister. Do you remember running as fast as you could with somebody gaining on you? Your breath is coming hard, yet you keep on running. A pain starts up in your side, yet the sheer exhilaration of the race keeps you going. At the finish line, you collapse on the grass. You won! Yes, you won! What joy! Giving is like that—the strange combination of effort, a painful stretching of yourself, leading to joy. Give till you feel the joy. Run the race set before you. Make a difference!

> *The Rev. Roy A. Cole*
> *Specialist for Revitalization*
> *Baltimore*

G-26

Receiving and Sharing, Life and Death

The Jordan River flows down from the mountains of the Holy Land into the Lake of Galilee, then flows out of that famous body of water, finally ending its journey by emptying into the Dead Sea.

Areas bordering the lake flourish with life, producing vegetation rich in beauty and ripe with food.

Areas bordering the sea, however, are quite lifeless, beautiful in their starkness, but barren of growing things.

Some would maintain that the lake receives fresh water from the Jordan in the north, but shares this gift with others by letting a portion leave from the south as the river resumes its journey.

They would also argue that the Dead Sea and surrounding shores are just that—without life—because this body only receives water, but never lets it go. There are no exiting rivers or streams from the Dead Sea.

That analogy could apply to ourselves. When we receive God's gifts gratefully and share a portion of them with others, our hearts will be flourishing, filled with life and deeply peaceful. On the other hand, hearts which only take and never share with others tend to wither, becoming lifeless and devoid of peace.

> *Rev. Msgr. Joseph M. Champlin, Rector*
> *Cathedral of the Immaculate Conception*
> *Syracuse, New York*

G-27

Giving

> You are being enriched in every way for all generosity, which through us will produce thanksgiving to God (2 Cor 9:11).

It was a bone-chilling day; the soup line moved slowly. The young woman blew on her fingers and stamped her feet as the line shuffled along. Finally, she was inside the door. Warmth and the wonderful smell of good soup and fresh bread lifted her spirits. As her gaze swept the room, her eyes fell on a sign, a small hand-written sign: "You are welcome, you are the guest of Christ." She bowed her head and gave thanks to this unknown one called Christ. Give so that others may give thanks to the One from whom all gifts flow.

> *The Rev. Roy A. Cole*
> *Specialist for Revitalization*
> *Baltimore*

G-28

Happiness

Happiness is not something we are given, but rather, something that results from the way we live. Happiness is a gift that comes from within; it comes from a life of generous giving of self. At the heart of achieving happiness is being what we all are called to be—grateful givers—sharing what we have received with the church and the poor.

Francis "Dutch" Scholtz, Director
Office of Stewardship
Diocese of St. Augustine

G-29

Giving and Receiving

Keep in mind the words of the Lord Jesus who himself said,
"It is more blessed to give than to receive" (Acts 20:35).

I know of a couple who gathered a church of homeless people in Las Vegas, Nevada, a town not known for its generosity to the poor. Each Sunday, in this little church, the offertory plate was passed with the words, "Give as you are able; take from it if you are in need." Each Sunday the plate was filled with dimes, quarters, and sometimes, a crumpled bill. No one took from the plate as it was passed. Each Sunday the congregation chose one of their own, the most needy, to receive the offering. In their giving of what little they had, they were blessed and were a blessing to one of their own. A mother of a sick child, who was given the offering one Sunday, wiped tears from her eyes as she said that no one had ever just given her money before. Thank you, God. It is truly more blessed to give than to receive.

The Rev. Roy A. Cole
Specialist for Revitalization
Baltimore

G-30

Grateful Giving

On Sunday, many of us offer simply what is left over or what has become a habit. A process of stewardship called "Grateful Giving" takes a different approach.

According to that procedure, we recognize that everything is from God above. Thus, whenever we receive a financial gift, whether from a weekly paycheck, our annual salary, a part-time job, our personal allowance, appreciation of investments, or a lottery windfall, we first thank the Lord, then take a portion (ideally, a tithe of 10 percent) and share it gratefully with others. This grateful offering is for building up the church and making this a better world: half goes to the parish and half to the poor.

Sacrificial giving makes God the top priority in our lives. In gratitude, we give back to the Lord a part of what we have received, only then keeping the rest for ourselves. Thus, we become "Grateful Givers!"

Rev. Msgr. Joseph M. Champlin, Rector
Cathedral of the Immaculate Conception
Syracuse, New York

G-31

Choices

> "No one can serve two masters. He will either hate one and love the other, or be devoted to the one and despise the other. You cannot serve God and mammon" (Matt 6:24).

The folklore of all peoples is filled with stories of fateful choices: persons finding themselves before two doors—one door leading to disaster, one to untold bliss. To avoid forks in the road like that Robert Frost paints in his famous poem which describes a crossroad illustrates a truth that our lives are determined forever by the choices we make. Week after week, we are offered a choice to declare ourselves to others and to our God, as to whom we belong—the small god mammon or the great God whom Jesus called Abba, Father. Choose wisely. Give to God that which God is due of the first fruits of your wealth.

The Rev. Roy A. Cole
Specialist for Revitalization
Baltimore

G-32

"To Give or Not to Give"

Shakespeare's Hamlet struggled with a mighty question: "To be or not to be?" We also struggle with our own mighty question: "To give or not to give?" The way of Jesus is not ultimately one of receiving but it is one of giving, the very giving of ourselves to the will of God. Discipleship is expressed in a life of stewardship—joyfully returning to the Lord a proportion of all that the Lord has given to us. Thank you for answering that mighty question: "To give or not to give?"

Most Rev. Robert F. Morneau
Auxiliary Bishop of Green Bay

Preparation of the Gifts—Special Occasions

SO-1

Air Conditioning

In many parts of this country, the summers are hot—hot and humid. We have become accustomed to air conditioning and it is a must if one expects the congregation to come to church and listen on 100-degree plus days.

———

This morning, outside, it is 101 degrees in the shade. But here inside we are comfortable, thanks to our air conditioning. We can worship without discomfort. I thank you for your offerings. Your gifts make it possible for us, as well as those who suffer health problems in the heat, to be here and join together to praise God. Thank you!

———

It is hot and humid outside. I give thanks for all of you who have come to worship here today in the name of Jesus in spite of the heat. I give thanks for our air conditioning that enables me to preach and you to listen to the Word of God. Your faithful offerings, week by week, enable us to pay [insert name of local utilities company] in order that all who suffer from the heat can join us, regardless of the outside temperature, to share in our Christian community. Thank you!

SO-2

Altar Guild

I recommend a public service of incorporation to the Altar Guild—those who care for this sacred place—this service represents a personal stewardship of time and talent and should be acknowledged.

Setting: Installation of Altar Guild members

This morning, we welcomed [insert names] as members of our Altar Guild. They give of their time to care for our sacred and holy things. It is one way that they practice their stewardship of time and talent. We are all called to give of ourselves to God through God's church and the world. Your generosity of time, talent, and treasure enables [insert name of church] to have a beautiful and moving worship. Thank you.

———

Setting: Sunday morning. (The altar looks especially beautiful.)

Each day, we come to worship here at [insert name of church]. This act is the center of all we do. However, sometimes we take for granted the lovely flowers, the shining communion vessels, and the immaculate altar area. I want to thank the members of the Altar Guild who come to clean, polish, and care for our precious, holy things. My thanks to all of you. Thank you, too, for your generous donations to our Flower Fund. Because of your stewardship, we have a beautiful place in which to worship.

SO-3

Altar Servers

In the Catholic Church we call the young men and women who assist the priest servers. After they have completed their training, we publicly install these servers. They are presented with a cross and a candle.

———

This morning, we have installed three new servers. It is a wonderful way that they choose to practice their stewardship of time and talent to serve Jesus Christ at his altar. I thank you for your practice of good stewardship that supports our youth ministry.

———

Every Sunday at [insert name of church] our servers serve Jesus Christ at his altar. They are faithful stewards who serve

Christ by giving their time and talent. This morning, [insert names] have been installed. Our thanks to all of you who practice good stewardship by giving of your time, talent, and treasure to support our children in this ministry.

SO-4

Baptism

Setting: Baptism Service

Today, we witnessed the baptism of [insert names] and we welcome them into our Christian community. We promise to do all that we can to support them in their new life in Christ. We do this through our weekly offering of our time, talent, and treasure. Some will teach them, but the money we all give will enable [insert name of church] to support [insert names] in their Christian life through fine religious education school materials, clean classrooms, and a welcoming Christian community. Thank you for your faithful stewardship.

————

Today, we all took part in an adoptive service. Through their baptism, we adopted these children into [insert name of church]. We vowed to care for these children as members of our church family. Your generous gifts of time, talent, and treasure enable us to do that. We are a welcoming Christian community that finds its identity in the name of Jesus Christ. Thank you for your generosity.

SO-5

Bible Study

Today, we gather to consider the stewardship of Scripture and our role as learners in the church. In practicing this aspect of our lives in service to God, we must exercise our willingness to "read, mark, and inwardly digest" the Word of God. This form of stewardship involves active engagement with others in discussion of biblical passages so as to relate them to how we live our lives each day. Our informed contributions to the discussion are essential to doing God's will in the world.

> *Dr. Amelia J. Gearey*
> *Virginia Theological Seminary*
> *Alexandria*

SO-6

Blood Drive

Once a year we have a blood drive in our church. This donation entitles everyone in the congregation to share in the Red Cross Blood Bank.

———

Some might say that we have taken stewardship to a *new low*. We have always talked about your giving your time, your talent, and your treasure to the church, but now, we want your *blood!* There is no way to make any kind of artificial blood. It cannot be purchased anywhere; it can only be given. We pray that you who are able to do so will come next [insert day] between the hours of [insert time], and give the blood of life.

———

Yesterday, [insert number] members of our church gathered in an act of stewardship—our blood drive. The money from our offering this morning is as vital to the church as that blood was for our community. It brings health to a world in need of God's love and reconciliation. I thank all who gave blood yesterday, and all who have given generously of their money this morning.

SO-7

Catechetical Sunday

We begin our religious education year with a simple liturgy for the dedication of the teachers, children, and parents to acknowledge their stewardship.

———

Setting: Opening of Religious Education Classes and Induction of Teachers

This morning, we took part in the dedication of our religious education teachers. They are giving of themselves, their stewardship of time and talent, to teach our children. Through your generous weekly offerings, we have the best materials available; clean, warm classrooms; and a giving, caring Christian community. With your offerings, we are caring for our children. I thank God for your faithful stewardship.

———

Each Sunday we have [insert number] children and [insert number] teachers gather for our religious education classes. We are indeed fortunate that many of our parents take their baptismal promises seriously "to raise their children to keep God's commandments as Christ taught us by loving God and our neighbors." Here at [insert name of church], our children are not our future, but our *present*. They bring life and God's love to us. Thank you for your generous offerings that enable us to share this "love of Jesus" with our children.

SO-8

Cathadraicum Tax

Each Catholic parish is expected to pay a cathadraicum tax of a fixed percentage of parish income to support the diocese.

Today, in my stewardship minute, I want to talk about our giving to the diocese of [insert name of diocese]. This year, we here at [insert name of church] are giving [insert amount] to further God's work and mission in the diocese. Part of every dollar you give in your offering goes to reach out and change the world in the name of Christ. I thank you for your generosity. When you read in your diocesan newspaper about all the good things being done in our diocese, remember—you helped make them happen.

As part of our church's stewardship of time, talent, and treasure, we here at [insert name of church] give our cathadraicum tax to the diocese of [insert name of diocese] because God has blessed us and we share our abundance with the diocese. This year we are contributing [insert amount], because God has blessed us. Remember, from every dollar you give and every dollar we receive for our budget, a share goes beyond these walls to change the world! On behalf of our bishop, I want to thank you for your generosity.

SO-9

Catholic Campaign for Human Development

Jesus invited us to prepare for the end of the world by facing and solving the problems of today's world. Time after time, Jesus showed us by his actions, and especially by his death on the cross and his resurrection from the dead, that he had come to overturn

the forces of evil and to restore life and dignity to those who suffer—most particularly to those who are victims of injustice.

Almost thirty years ago, the bishops of the United States offered a prophetic opportunity to Catholics in this country to
prepare for the fulfillment of God's Reign by addressing the problems of injustice and poverty through the work of the Catholic
Campaign for Human Development. During these years, the
Campaign has offered more than $250 million to organized
groups of poor people to bring about positive change in their
own lives and in our local communities.

Here are some examples of the accomplishments made possible by the Campaign for Human Development:

- a group of senior citizens has managed to obtain priority
  seating on buses and at bus shelters from their municipal
  transit authority;
- a community of Hmong refugees now can return to tradi-
  tional farming methods while, at the same time, they are
  building a thriving business which supplies Asian herbs and
  spices to local food stores and restaurants;
- groups of parents in various states have become actively
  involved in assuring quality education for their children.

Principles of good stewardship tell Catholics not only to be
generous in the annual Catholic Campaign for Human Development Collection, or through a share of your parish's stewardship program, but also to become actively engaged in resolving
the serious social problems faced in your local communities.

When Jesus comes at the time of our individual death or at
the end of the world, how will you react?—With fear and trem-
bling? Or will you be prepared and ready for Jesus' invitation,
"Come you blessed of my Father; you have built a more just and
loving world and can now live in the home of endless joy which
my Father has prepared for you."

Rev. Robert Vitillo
Executive Director, Catholic Campaign
for Human Development
Washington, D.C.

SO-10

Catholic Campaign for Human Development

If you and I had been casual bystanders some two thousand years ago when Jesus of Nazareth was preaching on this earth, we might well have concluded that he was a prophet who had things "backwards." After all, he thought the poor, not the rich, would inherit the kingdom. He insisted that the children, not the learned and clever, possessed the key to the great mystery of heaven. On the night before he died, instead of focussing on his own impending death, he knelt down and washed the feet of his disciples and assured them that they never again would be considered servants or slaves, but simply would be "friends" in God's new heaven and new earth.

About thirty years ago, when they established the Catholic Campaign for Human Development, the Catholic bishops in the United States asked us to follow the example of Jesus. At that time, in the late 1960s, our society was witnessing severe racial tensions and was watching the gap widening between the rich and the poor, between the "haves" and the "have nots." The bishops realized that, despite our church's admirable record in sponsoring hospitals, Catholic Charities, and schools, we had not yet succeeded in hearing the voice of the widow and the orphan or in letting the justice of God be done among the poor and those who were marginalized or oppressed in society.

Thus the bishops asked all Catholics to contribute to an annual collection for the Catholic Campaign for Human Development to support community-based, self-help groups in which poor people join together, learn leadership and business skills, and begin to participate in the democratic process in our society which so many of us simply take for granted.

Today Catholics in the United States can rejoice in the fact that we have gotten things "backwards" as Jesus did—by helping poor people to help themselves through the Catholic Campaign for Human Development.

Rev. Robert Vitillo
Executive Director, Catholic Campaign
*   for Human Development*
Washington, D.C.

SO-11

Catholic Charities

In the year 2002 Catholic Charities in the United States will be 275 years old! Our history begins with six Ursuline Sisters who came from France to New Orleans in 1727 with instructions from their superior to do whatever the community needed. They began a home for orphans, a refuge for "women of the streets," and a health-care facility for those wounded in the Indian Wars. From their care and concern and that of thousands of lay people, religious people, and clergy has grown the nation's largest network of local voluntary social services: Catholic Charities U.S.A. Their mission is to strengthen families, fight poverty, and build communities that care for the least among us. They thank you for your help, your time, and your financial support.

In 1997 Catholic Charities agencies across the United States helped 10.7 million people in need. 47,000 staff and over 250,000 volunteers fed the hungry, counseled troubled families, housed the homeless, protected children from violence in their homes, taught English to refugees, consoled the frail elderly, prepared couples for adoption, and taught job-skills to parents on welfare. Their work is an expression of our faith and an embodiment of Christ's mandate in Matthew 25: "Whatever you did to the least of my sisters and brothers, you did to me." We give thanks for your continued support of your local Catholic Charities agency.

Rev. Fred Kammer, S.J.
President, Catholic Charities of the U.S.A.
Alexandria, Virginia

SO-12

Catholic Church Extension Society
The Gift of Faith

Our beloved Catholic faith gives us strength and comfort. We express our gratitude to God for this faith in many ways. As we remember all of our loved ones in our future estate plans, we must also remember our beloved church. We want to "Give back to him." We can express our gratitude for the gift of faith by memorializing our love for the church through gifts in our wills and other estate plans. In making this commitment, we plan for the future of the church and give the legacy with the joy that comes from our faith. We are the caretakers of our faith and, as caretakers, we must advance the work of the church in the future.

> *Georgia Anderson*
> *Director of Planned Giving*
> *Catholic Church Extension Society*
> *Chicago*

SO-13

Catholic Church Extension Society
Responsibility for Faith

Here at the Catholic Church Extension Society we often use the words, "Extending and maintaining the Catholic faith in the poorest American Home Missions." As Catholics it is our privilege and responsibility to extend and maintain our faith in all circumstances and to all the people with whom we come in contact in our daily lives. In our examples of Christian charity, we are lead to be concerned for the future of our Catholic faith. To include a trust or a bequest in your will for your church is a gift of extending and maintaining the heritage of faith to future generations of Catholics. We thank all of you who have remembered the church in your will or trust.

Georgia Anderson
Director of Planned Giving
Catholic Church Extension Society
Chicago

SO-14

Catholic Schools

A Salute

Let me take this opportunity to salute Catholic schools. I regard them as a great gift to the church and to the country. There are 8,200 Catholic elementary and secondary schools across America serving 2.6 million students. During recent years, enrollment in Catholic preschools has increased by 223 percent—a testament to the fact that more parents are choosing for their children a Catholic education at an early age.

Numerous studies show that parents are supporting Catholic schools for three reasons: for the superior academic achievement of Catholic school students, for their secure and disciplined learning environment, and for their appreciation of morals and values. These reasons should interest you whether or not you have children of school age. Certainly, the future of our communities and of our churches depends on the ability and ambition of the next generation to pick up where we have left off.

Catholic schools have a track record of graduating students who are strong members of our church, as well as good neighbors and citizens. Most of our priests and sisters have had Catholic school training. Many of our civic and corporate leaders have benefited from a Catholic education. It is clear that our schools have played a key role in our Church in this country and in the very development of our nation as well. They are a gift, but they come with a responsibility. We must support and nurture these schools so that they can continue to flourish and be handed down to those who follow—just as these schools came to us as a cherished legacy of our faith.

> *Dr. Leonard DeFiore*
> *President, National Catholic Educational Association*
> *Washington, D.C.*

SO-15

Catholic Schools

Lighting the Way to a New Century

Nationwide, these days, Catholic schools across the country are using a common theme: "Catholic Schools: Lighting the Way to a New Century!" This slogan appears on many posters, brochures, and billboards. The message is that Catholic education is vital to the future of our church and our country. Why? Foremost is the fact that Catholic schools provide a value-based education. Morals and character count in our 8,200 Catholic schools.

During his recent visit to St. Louis (January 1999), Pope John Paul II celebrated Catholic education, commenting: "Catholic schools have proven to be of priceless value to generations of children, teaching them to know, love, and serve God and preparing them to take their place responsibly in the community."

Bishop Steib of Memphis, Tennessee, noted: "It is in the moral and spiritual environment of our Catholic schools that we build the kingdom of God in the hearts and minds of young people."

Emphasis on community is the foundation of Catholic schools—our faith community, the community in which we live. Studies show that students who graduate from Catholic high schools go on to become more involved in their faith and to serve as better neighbors and citizens. In this spirit, Catholic schools are lighting the way to a new century—a millennium made brighter by the strong character and morals of those who will guide us.

> Dr. Leonard DeFiore
> President, National Catholic Education Association
> Washington, D.C.

SO-16

Children and Worship

This comment discusses the importance of the responsibility of all Christians for teaching our children to worship.

———

Today, let us consider the gift of teaching another about God. We are called to share the message of the Gospel, yet many of us are not called to be evangelists. There is one very significant way that we can teach another person about God. Share your love of God with a young child. Teach children the love of God by welcoming them into your presence, even in church. Teach them how to worship by encouraging them to watch and imitate you in prayer.

> Dr. Amelia J. Gearey
> Director, Center for Teaching
> Virginia Theological Seminary
> Alexandria

SO-17

Children Are Wonderful!

How wonderful children are! They are gifts to me. They also are my teachers.

When I think of children, I smile. I raise my hands. I want to hug someone bigger than myself. I want to shout and sing! I want to laugh and dance!

God gives us so much for which we can shout and sing, laugh and dance! But it is the children in our lives and the child in all of us that know how to respond.

For all that God gives us, I want to shout THANK YOU! For all of the opportunities I have to respond by GIVING TO OTHERS from the abundance God has given to me, I want to sing and share! For all of the SPONTANEOUS MOMENTS that are invitations to "hug and dance," I want to praise God! For children, my teachers every day, I pray in GRATITUDE!

Sr. Rose Marie Hennessy, O.P.
Mission San Jose, California

SO-18

Children and Stewardship
Jesus, the Perfect Steward

Fostering stewardship among children should never be deferred on the assumption that they cannot comprehend its importance. To the contrary, stewardship is quite compatible with the values universally taught to the young during the formative years of their lives. Sharing and service, essential to the concept of stewardship, are not beyond the understanding of children, particularly if we expect them to grasp the legacy left by Jesus Christ. The younger members of our parish may well surprise us by their perception and response, especially as they develop a relationship with Jesus and grow to know him better as the perfect steward!

Rev. Francis W. Wright, C.S.Sp.
National Director, Holy Childhood Association
Washington, D.C.

SO-19

Choir Sunday—Blessing

On the last Sunday in June that the choir sings, we have the members come to the altar for a blessing of thanksgiving in appreciation for their leadership in praising the Lord.

———

At the end of the service this morning, we will ask our choir to come to the altar for a blessing, to thank them for their stewardship of their time and talent in leading us in worship every Sunday. We appreciate their faithfulness and dedication. I also want to thank you for your faithful and generous gifts of money each week. Because of you, our choir has new music, good robes, a quality organ, and a fine director of music ministries.

———

Each Sunday our choir leads us in praising God in joy for all creation. We appreciate the faithful stewardship of those who give their time at rehearsals and on Sundays and the use of their talent in singing and in playing instruments for the glory of God. We appreciate our music director, who takes responsibility for leading and supporting all those who are involved in our music ministry. We thank all who give of their time and talent. Today we will bless our choir. I want to thank you all for your generous giving. Because of you, we have a wonderful expression of your love and praise to God.

SO-20

Church Burnings

In the summer of 1996 many denominations and churches responded to the burning of the black churches in the South. These are two examples of how we addressed this problem with a special offering.

———

Today, as you open your bulletin, you will find a special envelope to help rebuild the black churches that have been burned throughout the South. We are now being given an opportunity to vote for justice and condemn this evil by making a generous offering of our prayers and money. I thank you for your generous weekly offerings, and I know, today, you will give to make a difference in our nation.

––––––––

This Sunday we have a special way to thank God for all the gifts God has so generously given to us and to stand with other Christians to rebuke those who have been burning black churches. Evil is with us and can be overcome only by God and godly people fighting for good. I thank you for your generosity in the past and give thanks for all of those who have made gifts and are making gifts for these people, to say we are one in Christ.

SO-21

Confirmation—Youth

We have a year-long preparation for youth who will be confirmed by the bishop. The entire parish supports their effort with time, talent, and treasure. Part of this preparation is the teaching of stewardship.

––––––––

Next [insert date], following a year of preparation, our youth confirmation class will be confirmed by Bishop [insert name]. I want to thank their teacher and all of you who, through your faithful stewardship of time, talent, and treasure, have supported these young people. These fine youth are a credit to our church. Thank you for your support.

––––––––

Today, I want to thank the members of our youth confirmation class for their stewardship of their time, abilities, and money here at [insert name of church]. They have worked hard to prepare for confirmation, giving of themselves and preparing to take on adult responsibilities within our church. We admire their dedication and commitment. I also want to thank you, the congregation, for your generous support. Your faithful stewardship, week by week, makes this day possible.

SO-22

Cursillo Weekend

Cursillo is Spanish for "short course." It signifies an ecumenical renewal program which is a short course in Christianity. It is a lay-led movement for mission, whose centerpiece is a three-day weekend, normally beginning on a Thursday evening and ending late Sunday afternoon. Those who are attending their first weekend are called candidates; those who lead the weekend are called staff.

———

Today, [insert number] members of our parish are attending a *cursillo* weekend. We will pray with them today. They are giving of their time and talent to experience a weekend of living in a Christian community. We give thanks to those who are sponsoring these candidates, giving of their time, talent, and treasure.

———

This morning our parish is sponsoring [insert number] members of our parish who are attending a *cursillo* weekend. A *cursillo* is a short course on Christianity. Our thanks to those who have supported these candidates through their stewardship of time, talent, and treasure. Our entire parish continually strives to become a strong, caring Christian community. Your generous offerings enable us to be such a community.

SO-23

Ecumenical

A growing number of local churches these days are committed to grassroots ecumenical cooperation through area ministerial associations and other groups. Through our stewardship, we support these cooperative ministries.

———

This past Monday our governing board approved a grant from our church to [insert the name and description of the specific group being assisted]. Together with other local churches we work there to proclaim the gospel by word and deed. I want to thank you for your faithful stewardship that enables us to serve those most needing our help. Your gifts of money each week really do make a difference in the world.

———

You know some of the good work that is made possible by your stewardship of time, talent, and treasure to [insert name of church]. However, many of you may be unaware of how we practice stewardship in working with the other churches in our area. We gather together through [insert own local church groups]. We are doing our mission by serving those in need in the spirit of cooperation, rather than acting in competition with the other churches. Thank you for your faithful stewardship that makes this possible.

SO-24

Evening Prayer

I bless the LORD who counsels me;
    even at night my heart exhorts me.
I keep the LORD always before me;
    with the LORD at my right, I shall never be shaken
      (Ps 16:7-8).

If we look out from this place, we know that the light of day is soon gone. We reflect on what has come to pass today. We anticipate an increase of darkness and quieting of our lives. In rest, we make our evening prayers thanking God for what has been today and asking for a good and holy night. As we rest in the peace of divine oversight of our night, may we count our blessings, remember opportunities for extending God's love well engaged. Yet also, we can with divine grace look forward to the dawning of a new day. May we recommit ourselves for tomorrow to new challenges and to face those things left unattended today that we may accomplish tomorrow. May the stewardship of our lives be accomplished for the sake of the good news of our Lord. End the day well and in thanksgiving.

The Rev. Ronald Reed
Pastor, St. James Episcopal Church
Wichita

SO-25

Fr. Damien de Vuester

Several years ago I traveled with a close friend to visit the island of Molokai, in particular, the section of the island where Fr. Damien de Vuester, a Catholic priest, labored and eventually died while serving the banished lepers of Hawaii.

In the nineteenth century, there was still vast ignorance about leprosy and no known cure. Hawaiians who contracted the disease were exiled to the island of Molokai, confined to an isolated peninsula that cut them off completely from the rest of the island. The colony had the reputation of being a graveyard and a lawless enclave of lawless people. The colony lacked police, medical care, sanitation, and dependable sources of fresh water. The lepers existed there in wretched housing.

A small group of Catholics pleaded with the bishop of Hawaii to send them a priest. Four young priests who worked with the

Sacred Heart Fathers in Hawaii volunteered to go and Father Damien was chosen. He arrived at the leper colony in the 1870s and began to organize the lepers to improve their living conditions. He came as a pastor of souls, but he soon became their doctor, nurse, engineer, builder, and accepted leader. He insisted on living and working in close quarters with the lepers so he could identify with them.

He built a chapel and imported an organ for Sunday services and provided other religious activities for them. Protestant members of the colony wanted a chapel of their own and managed to build one not far from the Catholic one. When they finished their chapel, they put up a plaque that read, "The following persons, abandoned by the human race, have built this chapel as a sign of our trust in God." The names of the planners and builders were written below this statement.

Father Damien then brought a hospital to the colony and established homes for the boys and girls of the community. Eventually, his labor for the lepers brought more substantial assistance in the form of long overdue supplies and services. At a Sunday morning Mass in 1885, he began his sermon by saying, "We lepers." He had contracted the disease of leprosy! He had given himself completely to the call and invitation to work for "those abandoned by the human race."

Someone has said that once we become disciples of Jesus Christ, stewardship is not an option. I believe this observation accurately describes the life of Fr. Damien de Vuester!

Most Rev. Sylvester Ryan
Bishop of Monterey

SO-26

First Communion

At our church, we have special Communion preparation in which parents meet with lay members and clergy for six weeks of classes in order that these parents may teach their children as a family unit. The children prepare a workbook and a scrap-book of their learning experiences, which they present at the offering.

———

This morning, [insert number] of our children will be receiving their First Holy Communion. As their stewardship, they will be placing their communion books in the offering plates. These books represent six weeks of their time and talent. The books will be placed on the altar and blessed and will be available for the congregation, as their extended family, to read at hospitality hour. As part of my stewardship, I will read them and write a personal response for each child. I thank you all for your generous giving that makes all of this possible.

———

For the past six weeks, our parents have been meeting for First Holy Communion classes so that they would be able to instruct their children about Holy Communion. I thank them for their stewardship of time and talent. They recognize that quantity time is no substitute for quality time, and they give generously of that. Our children will give their Communion books as their offering today. I want to thank the entire congregation for loving, accepting, and encouraging our children. The children know that they are loved here. Thank you for your generosity of spirit and money.

SO-27

Food Collection

We belong to an ecumenical agency that acts in our name for Christian charity. Our local group, called Assistance Center of Towson Churches, has a membership of forty churches. Each church takes a month during the year to provide for the food closet. We normally begin our month of supplying the food closet on Super Bowl Sunday, which we have renamed "Supper Bowl Sunday."

———

Today is Supper Bowl Sunday at [insert name of church]. As part of your stewardship, you have all been asked to bring in a bag of food to feed the hungry. Because of this stewardship, the hungry will eat during February. We give thanks for our youth confirmation class, who, as part of their stewardship, will collect this food and deliver it to the [name of charity].

———

Today, we are collecting food for the hungry. This is one way we practice our stewardship mission to feed the hungry and bring compassion to the world. Remember—no gift is *too large;* the food and money you give will bring life and health to our community.

SO-28

Funeral—Following Sunday

I believe Christians should be buried from the church. Today, since many of our parishioners are choosing direct cremation, a memorial service is held at the church.

———

On Thursday we buried Jane, a long-time faithful member of our congregation. Jane loved our Lord, and we trust that, with God's mercy, she now dwells with God in Paradise. Because of your faithful stewardship, we gave thanks for her life with a Christian Burial Mass. Your generous weekly offerings help us to have a warm and beautiful church in which her family and friends can come together.

———

On Thursday evening our congregation gathered to give thanks for the life of Charles. Charles loved the parish. He practiced exceptional stewardship in giving his time, using his talent, and generously sharing his resources with [insert name of church]. We will miss him. Our condolences go out to his family. His giving of himself strengthened our church.

SO-29

Garlic

As a child, I grew up during the Great Depression of the 1930s and World War II. As many other families did, ours had a beautiful vegetable garden, or as they were called, "a victory garden." My earliest and fondest memories were working in that garden with my grandfather.

Grandfather always planted many kinds of vegetables, but I was perplexed by his insistence each year that we must plant plenty of garlic. I noticed that my grandmother used very little garlic in her soups and other dishes. I asked my grandfather, "Why are we planting so much garlic? What will we do with all of it?" He always answered, "You wait. You will see!"

I watered and hoed around the many rows of garlic and cared for them and watched them grow. When they were finally ready to be pulled out of the rich, black soil, we would hose them down, and then my grandfather would tie them into elegant strings. After they were all lined up on the ground, I asked again, "Now, Grandfather, what will we do with so many strings of garlic?" His answer was simple. He said, "Take this string of garlic to your Aunt Petra, this one to your *madrina* Anita, this one to our neighbor Maria, and this one to my *comadre* Estela," and so on. Before I knew it, I had delivered all of the strings of garlic except one. "Now, this one is for us to take to your grandmother."

It was then that I finally understood why my grandfather had planted the garlic. It was one of the few things that he had that he could give to others. He had no money or other possessions, but out of the richness of his harvest he could share the blessings of God in his life.

As small children, we begin to develop attitudes of generosity. One of the first words we learn should be "share." I am sure many of you could relate similar stories of how you were taught about stewardship and the need to share the joy there is in giving. My grandfather responded with such pride and joy on sharing his bounty of garlic. We, too, can experience that same emotion when we give of what God has given us!

Most Rev. Ricardo Ramirez, C.S.B.
Bishop of Las Cruces

SO-30

Garlic

Cuando niño crecí durante la Depresión de los años 30 y la Segunda Guerra Mundial. Como muchas otras familias, la nuestra tenía un hermoso jardín de verduras, o como les llamábamos en aquel entonces un "jardín de victoria." Mis primeros y más bellos recuerdos son con mi abuelo en aquel jardín.

Mi abuelo tenía la tendencia de sembrar muchos surcos de ajo, y yo me quedaba perplejo por su insistencia de que cada año sembrarámos tanto ajo. Me fijaba que mi abuelo usaba muy poco ajo en sus sopas y otros platillos. Le preguntaba a mi abuelo, "¿Por qué estámos sembrando tanto ajo?" y el siempre me decía, "Ya veras, ya veras."

Yo tenía que regar y azadonar los surcos de ajo y cuidarlos y verlos crecer. Cuando por fin estaban listos para sacarlos de la tierra fértil y negra, los lavábamos y mi abuelo los amarraba en ristras elegantes. Cuando ya estaban todas en fila en el suelo, le pregunté una vez más, "Abuelo, ¿qué vamos a hacer con tantas ristras de ajo?" y su contestación fue muy simple. Me dijo, "Lleva esta ristra de ajo a tu tía Petra, esta a tu madrina Anita, esta a nuestra vecina María, y esta a mi comadre Estela," y asi sucesivamente. Sin pensarlo, ya había entregado todas las ristras de ajo excepto una. "Ahora, esta es para llevársela a tu abuela."

Fue entonces que por fin comprendí por qué mi abuelo sembraba tanto ajo. Era una de las pocas cosas que podía compartir con otros. El no tenía ninguna otra cosa, como dinero u otras posesiones. De la riqueza de su pequeña cosecha, podía compartir las bendiciones que Dios les daba.

Empezámos a tener actitudes de generosidad cuando somos niños. Una de las primeras palabras que aprendémos es "compartir." Estoy seguro que cada uno de ustedes puede contar historias semejantes de como aprendieron sobre la mayordomia, sobre la necesidad de compartir la alegría que se siente al dar. Mi abuelo respondio con mucho orgullo y alegría al compartir su abundancia de ajo. Nosotros tambien experimentámos esa misma emoción cuando damos de lo que Dios nos ha dado.

Most Rev. Ricardo Ramírez, C.S.B.
Bishop of Las Cruces

SO-31

Healing—Prayers

At every Mass at our church, we offer prayers of healing. Normally, we give specific names; we also mention those known only in the hearts of the worshipers.

Part of our stewardship is taking time, developing our ability to pray, to communicate with God in Prayers of Intercession for those in need of God's healing. In practicing good Christian stewardship, it is not time, or talent, or treasure, but all three, given to make known God's love for this world. We are healed, not to retire from God's service, but to serve God's world. We are always called upon to practice good stewardship.

Sometimes, in a conversation at school or work or at home, we are told, "I have cancer. I am going to have open-heart surgery. I am going through a divorce after many years of marriage." Many times, the response is: "I am sorry to hear that. Well, good luck!" For Christians, I believe that it is not luck, but prayers that make the difference. Next time, say, "I will keep you in my prayers." Do this as part of your stewardship. Pray for the person every day and at Mass on Sunday. It is a wonderful way to build a deep friendship with that person and with God.

SO-32

Healing Service

Every Wednesday at Mass, we have a service of Holy Eucharist and the laying on of hands for healing.

———

This past week I had the privilege of laying hands of healing, in the name of Jesus, on several of our parishioners. We here at [insert name of church] believe in God's power through Jesus Christ to heal body, mind, spirit, and soul. This is part of our stewardship of our gifts from the Lord. You are each present at this service. We remember the sick members of this parish and all of this congregation because, through your faithful stewardship, you are all a part of everything that this church does.

———

Do you believe in God's healing power? We do as a congregation here at [insert name of church]. Each time we celebrate the Eucharist, we proclaim by word and deeds the healing power of Jesus Christ. Whether you come on a weekday or Sunday, we *expect* Jesus Christ to heal, to bring his peace and comfort to those in need in body, mind, spirit, and soul. By your faithful stewardship, we stand here as a hospital for sinners rather than a country club for saints.

SO-33

Heritage Fund
Planned Giving

Our Heritage Fund is a perpetual fund, the income from which is to be used for repairs and major improvements to the church building and grounds. It is similar to the Endowment Fund in many churches.

———

Today, as part of [insert name of church] stewardship, I want to share with you an explanation of our Heritage Fund. This fund now has [insert amount] in assets. The income is used for the care of the actual church building and the surrounding property. We encourage our church members to remember [insert name of church] in their will—it is a way your gifts can care for our church buildings so that they will be here to minister to future generations.

———

Here at [insert name of church], we give of our time, talent, and treasure in many ways. Today, I want to thank all of those who have gone before us in this church. The Heritage Fund exists to care for capital funds and major improvements. Gifts are received through bequests and in memory of loved ones. They enable our buildings and grounds to be a fitting place for worship and ministry. I thank all who have remembered the Heritage Fund in their wills.

SO-34

Homebound Communions

I suggest that the name "shut-ins" be abolished and replaced with the word "homebound," which is more positive and descriptive. Monthly, I, my associates, and our eucharistic ministers bring Communion to our homebound members.

Each Sunday, when we gather to celebrate Holy Communion together, we set aside a part of the Body of Christ and save it in the tabernacle. Each week, Pastor [insert name] and our eucharistic ministers take the Body of Christ to the homebound. We share a simple Communion service and you are there with us. Thank you for your generous stewardship. Your offerings, given faithfully, enable Pastor [insert name] and me to be there in the houses, apartments, and nursing homes.

Each week, the clergy of [insert name of church] and our eucharistic ministers go out to the nursing homes and homes of our congregation and bring Holy Communion to our homebound members. At our church, we do not forget those faithful members who have left us a fine legacy of caring. Your faithful stewardship of your time and your talent, as well as your offerings of money, enable the clergy to be present with them. As part of *their* stewardship, our eucharistic ministers assist in this caring.

My thanks to you all.

SO-35

Hospital Calls

Calling on the sick, especially those in the hospital, is a top priority among all clergy I know. We believe that when we enter a hospital room, we bring the parish with us, for we go connected by prayer and it is through the members' generosity that we have the time to be there. All clergy have had the experience of representing almost a godly presence to those troubled souls.

————

This past week, I spent an afternoon at the hospital with the family of one of our church members, waiting for him to come out of surgery. I am happy to report that he is doing well and hopes to be home again soon. As I waited and prayed with the family, I thought about you and your stewardship. Your prayers sustained [insert name] and your generous offerings of time, talent, and treasure enabled me to be there. Remember when you hear that Pastor [insert name] was at the hospital—smile, feel good—for you were with me!

————

On Wednesday I drove to the hospital to make a call on a member of our parish. It is a huge, confusing place; it can be overwhelming. When I arrived at the parishioner's room, she smiled, tears welled up. I was a familiar face in the confusion and fear. While I shared Holy Communion, I thought of you last Sunday—how you came, prayed, praised, and gave your offerings and how, because of you, I could be there in that hospital room celebrating Holy Communion, sharing Jesus and you. Thank you. You are a special gift from God!

SO-36

Hospitality Hour

We no longer have a coffee hour St. Thomas', for two reasons. First, we not only serve coffee, but also tea, punch, juice, and doughnut holes. Second, and most important, we are serving Christian hospitality to all who come to worship at our Sunday service.

————

Each Sunday following our service, everyone is invited to come to hospitality hour, which is paid for by your generous stewardship. Your offerings make it possible. When you come and see a Sunday guest with a cup of tea, engaging in a lively conversation with one of our regular members, you are seeing the results of your stewardship. When you see children of all ages with their doughnut holes and smiles on their faces from ear to ear, that is your stewardship. Thank you for your generosity that makes [insert name of church] a growing, welcoming church.

———

Hospitality is an ancient Hebrew and Christian concept—that of welcoming the stranger. The Letter to the Hebrews tells us we entertain angels unbeknownst to us when we offer hospitality. Thanks to your giving of time, talent, and treasure, [insert name of church] is a hospitable church. We know that God wants us to reach out and welcome the newcomer. Thank you, for by your offering of yourselves, we are welcoming those whom God has brought to our church!

SO-37

Incorporation of New Members

I believe that every congregation needs to develop an incorporation service for newcomers—a liturgical way beyond confirmation to welcome individuals and families into the parish family.

———

Today, we welcomed and incorporated [insert number] new households into [insert name of church]. It is wonderful to have you all as part of our worshiping community and church family. We accept you as fellow stewards of our congregation. Together, we strive to practice good stewardship in the management of our time, talent, and treasure to build up the community of Jesus Christ.

———

It is wonderful to welcome our newest members to [insert name of the church] this morning. Our special thanks to our greeters who stand with me, at the back of the church, and to the welcoming committee who, as part of their stewardship of time, talents, and treasure, work to make our guests feel welcome. Your stewardship of time, talent, and treasure has made a difference. We are giving thanks to you.

SO-38

Labor Day

Setting: The Sunday of the last weekend of summer,
when we remember and lift up the value of work

Today, Labor Day has come to represent the last three-day weekend of vacation, the end of summer, and the beginning of the school year. Originally, Labor Day was a day set aside to appreciate those whose hard, physical labor made our nation strong. It was seen as a day of stewardship and an acknowledgment of the value of the use of our time, talent, and treasure. Our weekly offering comes from our labor. It is our way of acknowledging God, who gave us our stewardship over his creation.

———

Labor Day used to be a day of great parades in all the cities, as union members walked proudly before their families. Labor was seen as good—work that gave us the material necessities and comforts. But work is actually so much more than that. It embodies our share of creating in the world in which God has given us so much responsibility. We are all workers in God's kingdom. There is no retirement from discipleship. Our stewardship is how we manage all that God has given us. Your offering today of time, talent, and treasure is our human way of saying "Thank you!"

SO-39

Lazarus

We can look at things but never see them. We observe things but we do not pay attention. That is an old problem. Usually, it does not matter very much, but sometimes it matters a great deal. The rich man walked past Lazarus day after day and never noticed him. He was held responsible. In this parable, Jesus has the rich man sent to hell for not having paid attention. Surely, that mattered a great deal!

In this case, blindness is tied to feelings. We only really see what we have feelings for and we notice only those things we care about. If we do not care, we can not see. If we care about the poor man at our door, we will see him. We pay attention.

Individually, we cannot always help the poor man, but as a community, if we care, we can always see and do something. We are expected to support our communities so that they can reach out to others in need. The community is the Good Samaritan of which we all are a part.

Most Rev. Marcel Gervais
Archbishop of Ottawa

SO-40

Lazarus

Nous regardons, mais sans voir; il nous arrive d'observer des choses mais sans jamais vraiment leur prêter attention. Ce n'est pas nouveau. La plupart du temps, ce n'est pas vraiment important. Mais, il arrive que ce le soit. Dans la parabole de Lazarre, l'homme riche qui passait près de Lazarre tous les jours mais sans jamais le voir a été puni; il a jeté aux enfers pour ne pas avoir prêté attention a Lazarre.

Dans ce cas précis, on associe cécité et insouciance. On ne se préoccupe que de ce qui a de l'importance a nos yeux. Quand nous prenons soin du pauvre homme a notre porte, nous le re-marquons. Nous prêtons attention.

En tant que personne individuelle, nous ne pouvons pas toujours aider le pauvre homme, mais en tant que communauté, il nous est toujours possible de faire quelque chose. C'est pour cette raison qu'il est de notre devoir de soutenir notre commu-nauté, afin qu'elle puisse aider, tel un bon samaritain, ceux qui sont dans le besoin.

Most Rev. Marcel Gervais
Archbishop of Ottawa

SO-41

Legacies

The Bustle in a House
The Morning after Death
Is solemnest of industries
Enacted upon Earth.

The Sweeping up the Heart
And putting Love away
We shall not want to use again
Until Eternity.

Emily Dickinson

The bustle in the house the morning after death. The sweep-ing up of the heart. If I died tomorrow, or if you died, what would we be remembered for? What kind of responses would our lives bring to mind? What kind of legacy do we want to leave behind? Is it money or property? Attitudes or beliefs? Changed lives? What do we want to be remembered for?

I knew a woman who lived a very modest life and died a very wealthy woman. She wanted to leave everything she had to her college and to her church. And for this, she will be remem-bered. All those years, she was terribly worried that her money wouldn't last, and that all her life savings would be spent on nursing care. She was terribly upset. But in her last few days, a peace came over her and she seemed to shed her anxiety and fear. It was as if I watched her let go and move from this world to a place where she was free, where she didn't need to worry because God was in control, not she. I prayed for her and gave thanks to God for her legacy, but I wished that she had been able to trust God earlier and know the peace of God long before her death. I pray that each of us might know the peace that comes from faith in God long before—years before—the hour of our death.

> *The Rev. Phoebe L. Coe*
> *Pastor, Church of the Epiphany*
> *Odenton, Maryland*

SO-42

Legacies-II

> How to keep—is there any, is there none such, nowhere
> known some, bow or brooch or braid or brace, lace, latch or
>   catch or key to keep
> Back beauty, keep it, beauty, beauty, beauty, from vanishing
>   away?
> . . . Give beauty back, beauty, beauty, beauty, back to God,
>   beauty's self and beauty's giver.
>
> *Gerald Manley Hopkins*

What is it that we treasure so much that we are afraid to use it? Afraid to take it out of hiding and enjoy it, share it, use it? What kind of treasures and resources have you been given? What are you doing with them? What kind of legacy do you want to leave behind? Is it money or property? Attitudes or beliefs? Changed lives? What do *you* want to leave behind?

A few years ago my house was robbed. Among the items taken was a large gray flannel bag full of family jewelry that I had tucked away for safekeeping. Occasionally, I would take it out and examine its contents—trying on this, admiring that. It was only after the bag and all its contents were gone that I realized what I might have been able to do with those things. Actually, I could have kept them and always enjoyed them—if I had given them away! These inanimate objects could have been sold and transformed—silver and gold melted by God's love into instruments to help change lives. I wish I had done this. It is too late for that particular bag of treasure, but it is not too late for us. May we be able to give our treasures to God and God's purposes, for *really* safekeeping!

The Rev. Phoebe L. Coe
Pastor, Church of the Epiphany
Odenton, Maryland

SO-43

Mary, Mother of God
The Pieta

From the Presentation in the Temple until the Pieta beneath the cross, Mary made her awesome journey with deepest faith. As she held the lifeless body of Jesus in her arms, it was only her faith that gave her the courage to go on. It was with faith that she embraced Saint John as her son, since it was the wish of her dying child. Somehow, though perhaps only dimly at first, she came to understand that the suffering and death of her Beloved Son was the Father's will and would bring about the salvation of the world. Her faith's reward was the joy of experiencing his risen presence.

The Church lauds Mary as the Immaculate Mother of Jesus, but there is still more. The Church reveres her as its first and finest disciple, because of the depth of her faith. While yet under the cross, she received John the Divine as her child, as well. Indeed, in that moment, she embraced each of us who has faith in her son. Each one of us is privileged to call her "Mother."

Mother Mary, we pray that our faith may be strengthened especially in the difficult moments of our life. And, encouraged by your maternal love, may we strive to follow the Lord, as you did so valiantly.

Most Rev. James Keleher
Archbishop of Kansas City in Kansas

SO-44

Morning Prayer

> But the hour is coming, and is now here, when the true worshipers will worship the Father in Spirit and truth; and indeed the Father seeks such people to worship him (John 4:23).

The new day is celebrated in our morning prayers together. Another day is added to our lives for our enjoyment and use. We have begun this day well, because we have gathered to worship God and remember our relationship with our Lord. We are celebrating and cherishing this new day. It is a gift to us. And how shall we go forth from this house of worship this day? We are called by Christ and his church to carry the message of good news into our daily lives. How will our stewardship of this day unfold? Into what relationship, task, or fun will we carry this wonderful news? How can we take this daily gift of life and find a gentle application of Christ's love to build on the good news?

The Rev. Ronald L. Reed
Pastor, St. James Episcopal Church
Wichita

SO-45

Music

"Stained Glass Bluegrass Sunday" is an annual event when our choir teams up with a local bluegrass band to lead the congregation in the worship of God through the singing of many of the old (but rarely sung) songs that had their roots in nineteenth century revivalism and twentieth-century rural piety.

———

Today, we take literally the psalmist's encouragement to "make a joyful noise to the Lord. Break forth into joyous song and sing praises." Music and singing have always been among the ways that God's people have praised God and given expression to the joyful experience of God's grace in their lives.

Another way we give thanks to God is through our gifts and offerings. They not only make possible the ministry of music that enhances our worship Sunday after Sunday, but they also bring joy and hope to the lives of others through our local and denominational outreach ministries.

Therefore, with great joy and thanksgiving to God for all God's blessings, including the blessing of music, let us continue our worship through the giving and receiving of the morning offering.

The Rev. Mary Doyle Morgan
Pastor, Maryland Presbyterian Church U.S.A.
Towson, Maryland

SO-46

Novitiation—Bar Mitzvah

In the Episcopal Church this ceremony is like a group Bar Mitzvah. The Saturday evening before the bishop comes for confirmation, the entire youth confirmation class prepares and conducts the whole service of worship. Each candidate invites his or her parents, godparents, and friends with written invitations.

———

This is a wonderful evening for our youth confirmation class. We are proud of you! Thank you for leading us in worship, preaching the sermon, and praising God. Our thanks also to your parents, whose stewardship of their time, talents, and treasure brought you to [insert name of church] week by week. Sometimes church members may wonder: "Does my offering really make a difference?" Look around you at our confirmation class this evening. Is there any doubt? Thank you!

———

Tomorrow, Bishop [insert name] comes for confirmation. He will confirm the [insert number] young people who are leading our worship tonight. They are well prepared for this sacrament. Our thanks go to you for your faithful stewardship of time. Your children are here because you brought them. You have supported them by your example, your discipline, and your love. Our special thanks to their teacher, [insert name]. And our thanks, too, for your giving of money, for with your financial support, we have been able to act out of abundance.

SO-47

Nursing Homes—Services

One of the ways we serve the community is by conducting services at nursing homes. We receive no compensation for these services. This ministry is very important, but it is seldom held up as part of the stewardship of our members to help care for the world.

———

This past week, I thought of you all as I was leading worship at [insert name of nursing home], where each month in the church calendar, I visit and bring the sacrament we have shared and consecrated on Sunday to be shared with the men and women there. I preach and lay hands of healing on each one of them. I am able to be there because of your stewardship. The money you give each Sunday enables me to have the time to use my God-given abilities to preach and bring the love of Jesus Christ to those in special need of this love. Thank you for sending me. Your faithful stewardship makes it possible.

———

We all are aging every day, and some of us will spend our last days in a nursing home. Because we here at [insert name of church] want to reach out to those in nursing homes, we visit, hold services, and bring communion to both our local church members and nonmembers alike. This reaching out to help change our world is part of our vision, supported by your faithful stewardship. Your personal stewardship and our vision to "worship and serve in Jesus' name," enable me to be sent there. Thank you for your generous offerings and the gifts that make all of this possible.

SO-48

Planned Giving I
Outreach Fund

The Outreach Fund, begun by our previous pastor, is a model fund for those who do not want a general endowment to hurt good stewardship The income from this fund can be used only to help parishioners in need and for ministry outside the parish church.

———

Today, I want to share with you one of the ways [insert name of church] practices good stewardship—the Outreach Fund. This fund exists to help church members in financial need and the church's ministry beyond our own congregation. If you or one of our church members is in financial need, please speak to me. It will be held in strictest confidence. Our thanks to all who have made gifts and bequests to the Outreach Fund and to those who have mentioned it in their wills.

———

This past week, our finance chairman sent checks to various local ministries and community projects [insert name of groups]. This giving is part of our church's ministry to change the world. My deepest thanks to all who have made gifts to this fund and to those who have remembered the [insert name of church] Outreach Fund in their wills. Also, I thank you for your faithful Sunday offerings, for with these, too, we can work to change the world.

SO-49

Planned Giving II
How Will They Remember Me?

It is likely that many of us have probably been through the exercise of writing our own epitaphs. We see the announcement in the newspapers about someone we know who has died. Or we read what is said about a family member or an elderly person who has passed away, and we wonder what "they" would say about us.

What will they say about me? How will they remember me?

What is perhaps more important while I am still alive is for me to think about how I want them to remember me. How *I will* be remembered may, in fact, be a different question from how *I want* to be remembered!

Do I have time enough left in my life to do the things I should do and be the person I want them to remember me to have been?

Today is the first day of the rest of my life. What will it be from now on?

Fred Osborn
Director of Planned Giving
Episcopal Church Foundation
New York City

SO-50

Planned Giving III
What I Wish for My Children

I was privileged to be asked by the headmaster of my daughter's school to give a speech at the baccalaureate service before her graduation a few years ago.

In preparing for the speech, I found myself thinking rather profoundly about *what I wished for my daughter*. I thought of things like happiness, fulfilling relationships, an exciting job, that she have the chance to make a contribution to society, that she be a nice person and have a lot of friends.

And then I hit on what I really wanted for her—I want her to *be generous* for her *own* sake. I want her to feel the love that God and her family have for her. I want her to be able to confront the fear of not having enough (a fear that our culture is doing its damnedest to exploit!) and recognize that by *giving,* she will find deeper relationships and more lasting values. By becoming involved in organizations and causes bigger than she is, she will be on her way to finding herself in this huge, complicated world.

What do you wish for *your* children? What would you say in a baccalaureate speech at their graduation?

Fred Osborn
Director of Planned Giving
Episcopal Church Foundation
New York City

SO-51

Planned Giving IV
How Much Is Enough?

Our culture is filled with phrases that convince us that "just a little more" would be "enough." Indeed, the market economy under which our capitalist system thrives *must* establish a sense of scarcity in order to survive.

It has been said that the modern American dream is: to use money you don't have to buy things you don't need to impress people you don't even know.

Since we are bombarded with that message of scarcity day in and day out, can the church be the one place where, for a measly one hour a week, we talk about the abundance God has given us?

Can it be the place where we celebrate that God has given us "enough"? Isn't that what the gospel message is all about? "I am come that you may have life, and have it more abundantly."

That abundant life is here and now, revealed in how we look at what we have—recognizing our lives are as filled with gifts from God and from others; celebrating what we have, instead of complaining about what we do not have.

Generosity comes from the heart that is overflowing with a sense of abundance. It is to the generous that Christ promises the abundant life.

Fred Osborn
Director of Planned Giving
Episcopal Church Foundation
New York City

SO-52

Planned Giving V
Too Little Too Late

A very nice man came to me some time ago and said that he was worried about the continuation of his support to the church after he died. I suggested that he make a provision in his will for the church that would provide an income about equal to his pledge.

A year later, he came to me with the same concern. I asked him if he was happy with the way his will was written and he remembered that he had wanted to add the provision that we had talked about, but that he had not done so as yet.

A few months later, our church started its Legacy Club for members who have remembered the church in their estate plans.

I approached him to see if he would be willing to put his name
and picture on a letter to parishioners and talk about the Legacy
Club and what it meant to him. He said he was terribly embar-
rassed. He had fully intended to change his will to include the
church, but he just hadn't gotten around to it yet. He would get
right on to it!

That fall, he was diagnosed with terminal cancer. I did not
have the heart to ask him if he had "gotten around to it yet."
Nor did I have the courage to ask him if he were comfortable
with the provisions his will included. He died that winter.

It turned out that he had never gotten around to it. The tragedy
was not that the church did not receive the money. We will receive other funds from other sources. The tragedy is that this
good man, whose heart was in the right place, just didn't get to
do what he really wanted to do in continuing his support for an
organization that he really admired and wanted to help.

Fred Osborn
Director of Planned Giving
Episcopal Church Foundation
New York City

SO-53

Planned Giving VI
Managing Our Blessings

Those of us who recognize the blessings God has bestowed
on us are often quite aware of our responsibility to nurture, care
for, and "steward" those blessings. But what are we doing about
the use of those blessings after we no longer need them?

We recognize our responsibility to be stewards of our resources
while we live. But what about being a steward of those resources
after we die? If we are able, should we leave resources to continue caring for the things we cared for while we were alive?

Of course, first, we should make prudent provision for the
well-being of our families. *The Episcopal Prayer Book* directs the
minister of the congregation to instruct the people about that.

It also instructs people to make provisions, if they are able, to provide bequests for charitable and religious uses.

Have you made plans to manage your blessings after you are not around to manage them for yourself? Writing a will is not a difficult process. Getting to it seems to be!

You will feel much better when you have done it.

Fred Osborn
Director of Planned Giving
Episcopal Church Foundation
New York City

SO-54

Parish Newsletter—"Good News"

We send our church newsletter Good News free of charge to the entire church membership. We have a volunteer lay editor who does this as a part of her stewardship. I make sure that I read it before it is sent out so that I will know what is happening in the church and in the diocese. We send it twelve months of the year— the church does not take a vacation, only its clergy and the people do. The newsletter is sent out by a special mailing team.

———

This morning I want to give thanks for our parish newsletter editor and for our special mailing team, who are responsible for the newsletter's being published and delivered to our homes. This letter is especially appreciated by our homebound members, because it connects them to our church and they know they have not been forgotten. Our thanks to all in our church who give their time, talent, and treasure to make the good news of Jesus Christ known here at [insert name of church] and throughout the world.

———

Our parish newsletter is our way of communicating our life in Christ here at [insert name of church]. The newsletter doesn't just happen—it comes to your homes through the faithful steward-ship of our editor and our mailing team. They give of their time and abilities to make it happen. Our thanks to all of you who, through your stewardship of time, talent, and treasure, enable our church to be a church with good news to spread. Thank you!

SO-55

Prayer

How many of us have, at some point, thought that we would like to find more time for our prayer life, but we are just too busy?

Perhaps we would do well to ask ourselves the question: Whose time is it, anyway? With an understanding of stewardship, we would realize that it is all *God's* time. Time is a gift from God, and only God knows the total amount that we really have left. We have often heard about the three "Ts"—time, talent, and treasure. To be a true steward of time begins with the recognition that all time belongs to God and that our responsibility is to use it faithfully.

If it *is* God's time, how can we *not* spend at least a small sum of it in his presence through prayer? Making time to pray is, first and foremost, a decision of faith. Do you believe that, if you give time to God, then God will give you all the time you need? Do you believe that God's love for you is real? If so, your relationship needs your gift of time just as any other loving re-lationship does. Time in prayer is about putting yourself in the way of Jesus—the way of love.

It is God's time. Have faith. Make time to pray!

His Eminence William Cardinal Keeler
Archbishop of Baltimore

SO-56

Relief Services—Disaster

Catholic Relief Services are there for disaster relief, making grants on a national and an international scale to provide redevelopment after such disasters as the tornadoes in the Midwest and the war in Kosovo.

———

Today we are given the opportunity to make a special offering, above our weekly pledge, that will go to the Catholic Relief Services. We are called by Jesus Christ to care for those in need. Paul took a collection from the Greek congregations when those in Jerusalem were starving. Please be generous.

———

[Insert name of church] is committed to changing the world. We believe that if our church should disappear tomorrow, it would be missed and the world would be a poorer place. Today, through our stewardship, we have a chance to make a difference in our world. Our offering demonstrates our love and compassion for those far beyond our own congregation. I know you will be generous. Thank you!

SO-57

Religious Education—Year End Closing

On the second Sunday in June, we have a special service at which our children each make a class presentation and receive a pin—the Holy Spirit, a Cross, or another symbol—for participating in our religious education program. It is a gift of their stewardship of time and talent.

———

We applaud our children for their wonderful presentations this morning. They have practiced their stewardship of time and talent. We thank their teachers for their faithful stewardship, and we thank you for yours. By your offerings, our children have had the finest materials, clean and warm classrooms, and loving support in their learning. We all should feel good this morning, as we celebrate and give thanks for our children.

––––––

We give thanks for our children. Here at [insert name of church] we do not see them as our future, but as our present. They bring us life and joy. We thank their parents for sharing their children with us this past year. I thank you for your faithful stewardship. Your weekly offerings have provided our children with an excellent religious education program—the results of which we have experienced here this morning.

SO-58

Sabbatical

The church provided me two months for a sabbatical—two weeks in the Holy Land at St. George's College in Jerusalem and six weeks at Virginia Theological Seminary to write the first draft of this book.

––––––

Today, as I prepare to leave for [insert location], I want to thank you personally for my sabbatical. It is through your generosity that I am able to go to study, reflect, write, and refresh my ministry here among you. It is your stewardship and commitment to my growth and renewal that have made this possible. Please keep me in your prayers that I may make wise use of my time, talent, and treasure.

––––––

Tomorrow I will be leaving for my sabbatical, made possible by our governing board and your generosity in both spirit and money. I thank you for the faithful giving of time, talent, and treasure that you have invested in our future together here at [insert name of church].

SO-59

St. Ignatius Loyola
"Take, Lord, and Receive . . ."

A Meditation on St. Ignatius Loyola as a Model for Stewardship

In the Spiritual Exercises of St. Ignatius Loyola is this prayer:

> Take, Lord, and receive all my liberty, my memory, my under-
> standing, and my entire will . . . all that I have and call my
> own. You have given it all to me. To you, Lord, I return it.
> Everything is yours; do with it what you will. Give me only
> your love and your grace. That is enough for me.

"But pray it carefully," cautioned the priest who gave it to me.
"It will change your whole life!!"

Here, in this short prayer, is a blueprint for total stewardship. "You have given it all to me!" Ignatius says. The understanding that we do not own what we have is the first step towards
stewardship. It is the clear recognition that we are given all that
we have and are by God, in trust. Nothing is earned . . . it all is
a gift. The second step is the realization that we must be accountable for the use of those gifts. We ought, really, to return a
share in gratitude and to use the rest, all of the rest, wisely and
well. St. Ignatius passes that test: "Take it all!" he says. "Everything is yours. Do with it what you will."

For Ignatius, the surrender is total. Look carefully at all that
is being promised in that first sentence. "Take, Lord, and receive all my liberty . . ."

My *liberty*—my freedom to act, to think, to speak, to be.

My *memory*—my past and all I ever was or did or knew.

My *understanding*—my present and all that I know and believe and am today.

My *entire will*—my future and whatever I choose to be or do.

All of these—my freedom, my past, my present, and all that the
future might hold for me—"Take, Lord, and receive . . ." It is a
prayer that offers to return to the God of life and time, all claim

to that portion of life and time that he, in his goodness, has given to me.

I am awed by the scope and potential of this prayer to transform! Is it a prayer that I could pray honestly at this point in my life? What, if anything, am I clinging to that would keep me from praying it with sincerity? How might my life change if I could and did pray it?

Sharon Hueckel
Director, Pastoral Office for Development
Diocese of Lafayette in Indiana

SO-60

Seeker Service I

At the Community Church of Joy, there are special services for "Seekers"—those searching for a relationship with Jesus Christ through worship in the church. These services offer an alternative to the "Believer Services" of the Church of Joy. These mini-sermons are offered by Tim Wright, executive pastor of the Church of Joy, who is responsible for the worship at the Seekers' Services.

———

This past week, Joy conducted five funeral services—all of them for people who did not attend our church. They provided us with the opportunity to share the love of Christ with people at a time of loss and brokenness. Thanks to your faithful financial support, Joy was able to make a difference. Because of you, great ministry like this happens everyday. Thank you. Keep up the good work!

The Rev. Tim Wright
Executive Pastor, Community Church of Joy
Phoenix

The ministry of the Community Church of Joy exists because of the generous financial support of our members and friends. We do not get our funds from any sources other than our Sunday offering. It is your giving that enables us to provide excellent Sunday School classes for children, support groups, counseling, aid for those in need of food or clothing, and above all, exciting, inspiring worship. Your giving is making a difference. We encourage you to continue being a part of the great work God is doing through us!

> *The Rev. Tim Wright*
> *Executive Pastor, Community Church of Joy*
> *Phoenix*

SO-61

Seeker Service II

The Bible tells that God loves us so much that he gave his very best—he gave Jesus. In response to that great gift, we have the opportunity to say "Thank you" to God by giving him a portion of ourselves through our financial gifts each week. As we give, we honor God, and we participate in his mission of letting others know about Jesus.

> *The Rev. Tim Wright*
> *Executive Pastor, Community Church of Joy*
> *Phoenix*

———

At this time, we are going to receive the offering. This is the time when the members and friends of Joy, through their giving, help underwrite and support this ministry. If you are visiting with us today, we want you to know that you are under no obligation to participate in the offering. You are our guests. We are glad that you are here and we invite you to join us again just as soon as you can. To those of you who are family and friends of Joy, we want to invite you to continue your generous and faithful support.

The Rev. Tim Wright
Executive Pastor, Community Church of Joy
Phoenix

SO-62

Serving

It is wonderful to see people come to church! Most are filled with devotion and expectations. We come to church wanting things to be right. This attitude, however, can easily allow us to slip into one of coming to church "to be served."

We are so much a part of a consumer society that we sometimes develop an attitude of going to church the same way we go grocery shopping. It is just one more thing to do. There is only one way to cure this attitude of consumerism in church: that is, active participation in the life of the church itself.

It is the same with our families. If grown children simply take whatever they can get from their parents and never give to the life of the family, they eventually find themselves outsiders, looking in.

One who participates in the family and one who participates in the life of the church is one who contributes his time, talent, and treasure to them and one who receives innumerable blessings in return.

Most Rev. Marcel Gervais
Archbishop of Ottawa

SO-63

Serving

C'est merveilleux de voir les gens à l'église. La plupart sont remplis de devotion et d'espérance. Quand nous venons a l'église, nous nous attendons à ce que tout soit parfait. Cependant, cette attitude peut facilement déraper en une attitude d'attente.

Nous vivons tellement dans une société de consommation que nous allons même à l'église de la même façon que nous allons faire nos emplettes, soit pour obtenir le mieux possible au moindre coût. Il existe cependant un antidote à cette attitude, et c'est la participation à la vie de la paroisse.

La même chose ce produit dans nos familles; les enfants, devenus adultes, ne font que reçevoir ce leurs parents sans ne jamais rien donner en retour, éventuellement, ces enfants n'auront plus leur place au sein de cette famille.

Participer activement à la vie de sa famille, de sa paroisse, signifie partager son temps, ses talents, et ses trésors avec les membres de cette famille, de cette paroisse.

Most Rev. Marcel Gervais
Archbishop of Ottawa

SO-64

Serving the Poor

My wife Joan and I received the call to serve the poor in 1975. We gave away all of our possessions except our home. Since that time, we have kept no savings accounts, no life insurance, no retirement funds, no savings bonds. We do not own cars.

I still practice medicine and received my post graduate training at Harvard Medical School in dermatology. Jesus is true to his word. If we trust him, he will shower us with riches beyond those of the human world. He has done this for our family!

As we work for the poor, we find that though we often become tired, our benefits far exceed our fatigue.

> *Andrew A. Simone, M.D.*
> *Executive Director, Canadian Food for Children*
> *La Nourriture du Canada les Enfants*
> *Toronto*

SO-65

Sharing

The world we live in tries to make us selfish! For most of us, I believe it has succeeded. It is difficult to have faith and to believe sincerely that sharing all of our financial goods along with our talents and time would really benefit us since it would take away from our possessions.

My wife and I are just back from El Salvador where we met a little girl, Jennifer, who, at the age of twenty months, weighs only thirteen pounds and five ounces! Because we shared our worldly goods, Jennifer will have a chance to recover from her malnutrition. I believe that is what Jesus meant when he said we should love one another!

> *Andrew A. Simone, M.D.*
> *Executive Director, Canadian Food for Children*
> *La Nourriture du Canada les Enfants*
> *Toronto*

SO-66

Soup Kitchen

Through our Love Boxes, Outreach Fund, and volunteer efforts, our church supports an Episcopal-Ecumenical Soup Kitchen in Southwestern Baltimore. We now make box lunches for one hundred people each month.

Today, I want to share with you one of the fine Good Samaritan ministries we here at [insert name of church] support through our stewardship of time, talent, and treasure. Through your generous offerings, the homeless and hungry of [insert name of city or town] will eat this week. Jesus told us to feed the hungry and we are doing that because of your generosity.

———

This past week, a group of eleven volunteers went down to Paul's Place to prepare and serve lunch and then to wash up, clean the tables, and sweep the floor. In your name, we looked into the eyes of the hungry and, on your behalf, we received many heartfelt "Thank Yous!" You should feel good about this ministry—it is an outgrowth of your generous giving. Thank you!

SO-67

Stewardship Sunday

On Stewardship Sunday the parishioners are asked to bring their pledge cards to church and, as families, bring the cards when they come forward for Communion. Stewardship Sunday is a joyful day of worship.

———

Today, when you come forward for Holy Communion, please bring your pledge cards with you and place them in the alms basin, which will be here in the middle of the chancel. Our commitment of our pledge of money is an acknowledgment that all we have is a gift from God, and we are choosing to honor God by returning to him a portion of what we have received for the work of Jesus Christ through our church. Thank you for your commitment to God through [insert name of church].

———

Today, we celebrate and acknowledge with thanksgiving all of God's gifts to us. We are honored to make our commitment to God's work for next year through [insert name of church]. We joyfully acknowledge the source of all goodness and life, and respond by our offering of our pledges this morning as we come forward to receive the Bread of Life. Thank you for your faithful stewardship.

SO-68

Stewardship
A Good Steward?

As a practicing Catholic, helping out at the church and tithing, I felt I was doing just about everything that was expected of me.

Stewardship? Sure, I knew what stewardship was. To me, stewardship meant a regular review of my department by the management of the company where I worked. Stewardship in the church? Well, I had heard the story of the good steward and that was about it. I decided that stewardship was almost a synonym for tithing.

Then, I met Andrew and Joan, a remarkable couple actually living their lives in a way that was different. They helped me to understand what "stewardship as a way of life" really means.

Their journey along this path began in 1975 with a conversion experience, when they discerned a call to dedicate their lives to helping the poor. They gave away nearly all of their money and possessions, keeping only their house for their thirteen children and the twenty-six foster children they took in over the years!

Then they founded an organization that sends over five million pounds of food to starving children in over thirty countries in Central America, Africa, and South America. Andrew keeps up his medical practice on a part-time basis to help raise funds for the charity and support their frugal lifestyle.

Becoming a steward does require a conversion! Perhaps it would not be as radical a one as that of Andrew and Joan, but a conversion, nevertheless. One must experience a conversion that makes one see the world and those in it, including oneself, in a totally different way!

This couple gives us a powerful example to follow.

Terence T. Thompson
Director of Stewardship and Development
Archdiocese of Toronto

SO-69

Stewardship

How's Your Scorecard?

Recently, I was chatting with a friend who had come to this country a few years ago from a place that was very different from our country. I was reminded of our freedom and of our many, many gifts here in America.

In the country he had left, my friend told me that he needed a card to do virtually anything. Either his card was marked for each trip or event or a special pass had to be issued . . . if he could qualify! His cards and papers told the story of his restrictions and privileges and, in a way, his life. He had to produce them at any time, and he had to prove that he was in the right place, doing the right thing.

What if we were issued a card to record all of our gifts: the gifts we were issued when we arrived on earth and the ones we have been given by our Lord as we journeyed through our lives? In most cases, we were born free, in good health, expecting a life span of eighty years or so. Most of us have ample skills to get through life and we have our faith, a special gift that "sets us apart." Some of us are specially gifted with exceptional talents to be highlighted as a bonus, for special review!

Imagine that this card will be marked to record all of our acts of good stewardship: the use we make of the time given to us; the use of our life skills and any special talents we have been given, including our faith; the use of our treasure. Will our card show that we used the first fruits of our labor for ourselves or for the Lord? Will it show that we gave sacrificially? Will it show that we helped those who could not care for themselves or those who needed special words, deeds, or love?

When you hand in your card to St. Peter and ask for your room in the house of many mansions, will your card admit you? Our Lord is kind and gentle and forgiving, but he demands much of us. As the Scriptures say: "Much will be expected!" He sets high standards. Shouldn't you?

Terence T. Thompson
Director of Stewardship and Development
Archdiocese of Toronto

SO-70

Stewardship

It's Not Mine!

Stewardship, the word, is one of those terms that we as Catholics immediately dismiss by claiming:

a. It is too Protestant!

b. It is just about money!

But if we get past the term into the true meaning, we find that it is not really a term at all, but rather a lifestyle, a lifestyle which sets priorities for ourselves.

How do we want to spend our time? How do we plan to use our talents? How do we distribute our wealth? Before we make these decisions, we must first decide if we really want to be disciples of Jesus Christ. If not, then how we spend our time, talents, and treasure does not really matter. BUT, if we truly want to live as his disciple, stewardship is not an option.

In America, we enjoy enormous wealth . . . Do not look at your neighbor . . . you, me, the vast majority of us have more than we will ever be able to use. And it is NOT OURS! It belongs to GOD! We are but his managers.

So, give back to God what is his already. Feed his hungry, clothe his poor, love his children, protect his environment, and manage his wealth!

Sandy Ferencz
Director of Stewardship and Development
Diocese of Charleston

SO-71

Stewardship

It's Your Own Business

I was a very young pastor working with a fairly new stewardship committee. We were altogether determined somehow to reach those families that never pledged or that never kept up with a pledge. The stewardship consultant we approached was of no help to us in this at all. He even said to us that we were working on the "wrong" people. He had the gall to say that we should first of all start with ourselves! Good Christian stewardship does indeed begin with ourselves. It begins with "Me!" It is "My business!"

It is the heavenly Father's business. "All things come of thee, O Lord, and of thine own have we given thee."

The Rt. Rev. C. L. Longest
Episcopal Suffragan Bishop of Maryland
Baltimore

SO-72

Stewardship

Let Go!

Stewardship is a way of life that helps the Christian "let go" of the things of the world while still earning a living . . . making payments on mortgages . . . paying school tuitions and insurance policies!

It surely helps us to let go, especially with greater security. But it does so much more. It is a way to counteract the materialism, consumerism, and individualism which are the antitheses of the culture of love in the home, the Church, and the community.

Stewardship builds the civilization of love by hearing God's word and putting it into practice. It insists that the Christian must do good and not be content with a faith that produces nothing.

Stewardship recognizes that God is the one who gives us all these gifts, blesses them, and produces the increase that we experience when we place ourselves at the service of one another.

Most Rev. Eugene J. Gerber
Bishop of Wichita

SO-73

Stewardship

Magnets

Stewardship and life are like two magnets. Each has a positive and negative force: positive, because one has been a part of the other from the foundation of the world; negative because original sin places them in diametrical opposition. As life and stewardship draw towards each other, as intended by God from the beginning, the field of attraction becomes more powerful. Eventually, the person and God rest in each other as two magnets do.

When stewardship and life go in opposite directions, the opposing forces create disturbance within us, around us, and beyond us. They propel us away from God, our very selves, and the whole of creation.

The creation story, the incarnation story, the salvation story, all of these show us the way to bring stewardship and life together so that the forces of good bring rest to our souls and the souls of others.

Most Rev. Eugene J. Gerber
Bishop of Wichita

SO-74

Stewardship

The Real Meaning

Close your eyes. Take a deep breath.

Now, think of the word "stewardship." What does it mean to you? What words could describe your inner feelings about stewardship? A dreaded obligation? A burdensome contribution of money? An odious duty of the baptized? Or a love-filled sharing with all of God's people? A blessedness granted to the poor in spirit?

We want to feel the later about stewardship, but too often it is the former. The pace of our lives is so hectic. We have so many obligations and worries that finding the will to share time, treasure, and talent is often more than we can cope with. When the children are gone and settled in their own adult lives, we say, then we can be good stewards. When we are retired and free, then we will be the best stewards the church has ever had! When I get that promotion, then I will have the wherewithal to get serious about caring for God's people and the world! But right now, our spirits are too anxious. We are too burdened even to think about stewardship.

But have we forgotten that THIS moment may be the only moment we have? To be baptized means to live each moment as one of Christ's moments. So today, this moment, can we not open our minds and hearts to let the Lord's pure love overwhelm us? Can we look at stewardship not as a dreaded obligation, but rather, as a personal invitation to love and care and share with others. Our faith tells us that his overwhelming love will free our spirits from fears and apathy, enabling us to soar in his love!

Dr. Elinor R. Ford
Fairview, North Carolina

SO-75

Stewardship

Oh, Lord, I am not Gifted Enough to be a Steward!

Directions to the homilist: *Fill a tall, thin bottle and a small, squat bottle with the same amount of water. Both bottles should hold the same amount, but look as if they hold very different amounts of water. Have two identical glasses into which the water can be poured.*

———

Look at each of these bottles. Which one holds the most water? Which one holds the least? (Now, pour the water from each of the two bottles into the two glasses and hold them up so that the congregation can see that each holds the same.)

Surprised? Look around at each one here. Do we look the same? How do you feel about yourself? About others in the congregation? Some are tall. Some are small. Some are young. Some are old. Some are richer, while others are poorer. Some appear to be gifted, but others seem very ordinary.

But when we are poured out for our heavenly Father who created each of us to be unique and who has given each of us a very special life mission, are we not equal in his sight? We cannot hide behind the excuse of not being gifted enough to be involved completely in our church's stewardship mission. Instead, we need to go home today and reflectively and prayerfully write out the life mission to love and care and share that God has given each of us. Then we need to write out one way that we will live out that mission in the coming week. When we have done that, we will know that though we appear to be less gifted, less talented, less famous, or less wealthy than others, when we pour ourselves out as God's stewards, we are indeed equal in his sight!

Dr. Elinor R. Ford
Fairview, North Carolina

SO-76

Stewardship

The Appreciation of God's Abundance

John 6:1-15

In his Gospel, John shares with us the wonderful story of how Jesus fed 5,000 hungry men with the two fish and five barley loaves that a small boy gave him. Jesus took the loaves and the fish, gave thanks, and not only was able to feed the thousands that were there with him, but also, he had twelve baskets of barley loaves left over, a marvelous sign of God's abundance.

I see ourselves as the boy in the story, giving to Jesus our time, talents, and treasure, however small they may be. Jesus receives them, blesses them, and accomplishes so much more with them than you or I could ever imagine!

What a wonderful Jesus, who takes and appreciates our gifts, multiplies them, and makes it possible for us to be his eyes, ears, mouth, mind, hands, and heart, empowering us to serve him in the world for which he sacrificed his life on the hard wood of the cross.

SO-77

Stewardship
Through a Lens

Consider stewardship as a contact lens. A contact lens is a thing unto itself: it has mass. I can look at it and consider it. But its true function is not revealed until I put it into my eye. That function is to be a filter through which I view the world. When I have a contact lens on, I look right at it, but I cannot see it. However, once I begin to wear it, I see the world in a whole new way! With my contacts in, things become clear. I am able to move through the world and to perform my activities with greater confidence. I am even able to see things which I could not see without my contacts. Once I begin wearing these lenses, the world is truly a different place!

Stewardship is a thing unto itself. It is a clearly defined group of ideas. However, its true power is visible only when we use it to interpret other things. Once we are aware of it, we see more clearly and act with greater confidence than ever before, because now, we are doing God's will!

Greg Bowden
Director of Annual Appeal
Diocese of Charleston

SO-78

Stewardship
Way of Life

The stewardship way of life is the total life response of the Christian who has been touched by God's love. We can decide whether or not to accept or reject Christ, but once we accept him, stewardship is no longer optional. We have become stewards of God's gifts which he has given us freely. Stewardship is love. Stewardship is thanksgiving. Stewardship is sharing.

Stewardship is all of us doing our share to fulfill God's mission and stewardship will lead us to heaven.

The stewardship way of life teaches us that we must be thankful people and return to God a proportionate amount of the time, talent, and treasure that he has so graciously given us. Stewardship is a "faith journey" along the path of life. Because all gifts come from God, we must use those gifts in a responsible manner to promote his kingdom on earth.

Rev. Msgr. Thomas McGread
Pastor, St. Francis of Assisi Church
Wichita

SO-79

Stewardship Witnesses

On the Sunday preceding Stewardship Sunday, at both of our Sunday morning services, we have two lay persons witness to their practice of stewardship.

———

This morning, I want to thank [insert names] for witnessing to their personal stewardship. It was gratifying to hear how they and their families are giving out of grateful hearts in thanksgiving for all of God's blessings. During the coming week, you are being asked to pray about your financial stewardship to God through your church family. Your decisions will decide the future of our parish for next year. I pray that we are becoming a tithing church and that we may continue to have the resources to proclaim Jesus Christ as our Lord and Savior.

———

You have heard the witness of [insert name] and [insert name]. Later this week you will receive a letter with a pledge card and envelope from our stewardship chairman. I ask you to pray alone or as a family about your pledge to God for [insert year] through [insert name of church.]

What you commit to God's work here will decide the future of your church. Will we continue to reach out in the name of Jesus and grow, or will we be held back and shrink? The choice is yours. May God, through the Holy Spirit, guide you in your decision this week. Next Sunday we will gather and give thanks for your pledges in a service of celebration and thanksgiving.

SO-80

Theological Education
Ecumenical/Lay
Leadership

The Ecumenical Institute of Theology at Saint Mary's Seminary in Baltimore is dedicated to master's level theological education for personal enrichment and to preparation for lay ministry in the various Christian churches. In the twenty-first century, the number of significant lay leaders (including diaconal ministers and lay pastors) is going to increase in every denomination, although for reasons peculiar to each tradition. The question before us is whether such leadership will be excellent or mediocre. Without good theological education for the laity, more often than not, the answer will be "mediocre." Our thanks to all who through their stewardship of time, talent, and treasure are strengthening our education for the laity.

Michael J. Gorman, Ph.D.
Dean, Ecumenical Institute of Theology
St. Mary's Seminary
Baltimore

SO-81

Theological Education
Ecumenical/Lay
Vision

A steward is someone with vision. Today, we give thanks to God for stewards, for people of vision, for people who see what might be, who want to help God create something out of nothing. For more than thirty years, it has been the visionary stewards who have created programs, served on planning committees, started and enhanced endowments, and gradually added to the spiritual and financial health of this institution. Their vision for lay education and for lay ministry in the church means not only that this school prospers but also, and more importantly, that the work of God is advanced. Thanks be to God for this unspeakable gift!

Michael J. Gorman, Ph.D.
Dean, Ecumenical Institute of Theology
Baltimore

SO-82

Theological Education
Ecumenical/Lay
The Widow's Mite

One of my favorite stories in Scripture is the one often referred to as "the widow's mite." It is told by Luke in four short verses in his twenty-first chapter, and it contrasts sharply the rich who give to the temple treasury out of their abundance and the poor widow who gives two small copper coins out of her poverty. According to Jesus, she gave more than the wealthy did. Today, I am grateful to the many benefactors of the Ecumenical Institute of Theology who give not a thousand dollars annually, but only five or ten dollars. These include a number of women in religious life. When I offer my "thank you" to each of you, know that I do so with deep respect and sincerity.

Michael J. Gorman, Ph.D.
Dean, Ecumenical Institute of Theology
Baltimore

SO-83

Tithing I

Tithe, a five-letter word, is as close as you can get in the Christian church to a four-letter word—mention it and Christians rise up in protest! However, if you teach it, it will make a difference in the lives of your church members. It is best, however, to talk about this at a time that is not related to Stewardship Sunday.

———

Each Sunday we pass the collection baskets and give our offerings. The question we all need to answer for ourselves and our families is: "How much should we give out of all that has been given us for his work?" Our church uses as the standard "the biblical tithe" as the minimum for our giving. I pray that the standard is our standard now, or that we are moving toward that tithe. Thank you for your disciplined giving, week by week, for God's work through [insert name of church].

———

In a few moments, the ushers will pass the collection baskets among us and in them we will place our offerings to God. I want you to consider the tithe as the minimum standard for giving to carry out God's work. We believe we are doing God's work here. We ask you for generosity, in a disciplined way, to support us that we may continue this task. Thank you for choosing our church as your primary way of returning to God a portion of what has been given you.

SO-84

Tithing II
Good Stewards of All God Has Given Us

God is the source of all things. God calls us to be accountable, as any steward is accountable, for all the things that God has given to us. We are accountable for 100 percent of all that we have in our possession. That means all of our time, our talents or gifts, and our treasure. Tithing helps us to manage better that 100 percent. To be able to tithe absolutely requires that we learn to manage well all that we have and all that we are. Every one of us can learn about money, about ourselves, about God as we grow in our ability to be good stewards of all that God has given us.

> *The Rt. Rev. C. L. Longest*
> *Episcopal Suffragan Bishop of Maryland*
> *Baltimore*

SO-85

Vision—Church

The Vision Statement of our church reads:

> We are a church of Jesus Christ, in which all people are welcome, every member is a minister, the world is our responsibility, disciple-making is our goal, and worship is our duty and delight.

We cannot accomplish any part of our Vision Statement without your generosity. When joining the church, we pledged to "faithfully participate in the church's ministries by our prayers, our presence, our gifts, and our service."

Thank you for your past gifts, and let us look forward to the wonders that can be accomplished by the guidance of our Vision Statement and our giving our offerings through love.

> *Catherine A. Ritter*
> *Director of Family Life*
> *Towson United Methodist Church*
> *Towson, Maryland*

SO-86

Wedding—The Following Sunday

In the Catholic Church, a couple normally is required to attend premarital counseling preparations, then the wedding rehearsal, and, of course, the wedding itself.

———

Yesterday, I witnessed and blessed the marriage of [insert names]. It was a joyful day! I thank you for your faithful stewardship that enabled them to meet for premarital counseling sessions, have a wedding rehearsal, and then to gather here yesterday with their family and friends. They came here as strangers, and through your love and acceptance, they have become members of our church family. Thank you again for your generous gifts, for you are building a Christian community.

———

Yesterday, here at our altar, [insert names] had their marriage witnessed and blessed. They know that this is their spiritual home. Thank you for your generous gifts each Sunday. Your giving enabled me to be available to meet with them to prepare them for their marriage. Your gifts provided a beautiful, holy place for them to gather yesterday and celebrate this event. Your faithful gifts of time, talent, and treasure are building a Christian community. Thank you!

SO-87

Welcoming Committee

Our Welcoming Committee is responsible for welcoming all who come as strangers to [insert name of church]. They act as greeters, stand with the clergy after services, take pictures of newcomers and post them on our Newcomers' Bulletin Board together with brief biographies, and act as "buddies" to new families, introducing them to the rest of the congregation. All but one of them have been in the parish for less than three years, so each one can easily remember what it was like to be "the new kid on the block."

———

Today, as part of our stewardship, I want to thank our Welcoming Committee members here at [insert name of church]. They meet you after the service, standing next to me at the door. They take the pictures for our Newcomers' Bulletin Board, and their special ministry is welcoming the stranger. But we realize that welcoming the stranger is part of *every* baptized member's ministry. This is one significant way we here at [insert name of church] practice our stewardship of time, talent, and treasure. The five-year-old child reaches out to a new child in kindergarten class. You greet someone new after church or visit over a cup of coffee during hospitality hour. These are the ways you serve, and you are the reason that our church is growing. Thank you.

———

This morning, [insert name] will be taking pictures of our newcomers for the Newcomers' Bulletin Board. We are thankful for all those whom God is bringing to our church "to worship and serve in Jesus' name with us." I thank you for your faithful stewardship of your time, talent, and treasure. By your generous giving of each, you are helping [insert name of church] live out its mission. Thank you!

SO-88

Wills and Bequests

Today, I want to remind each member of our parish that you need to have a will. It is your responsibility to care for your family. As you are part of our church family here at [insert name of church], I pray that you will also remember us generously, as much as you are able to do so.

———

A will is your final statement of your Christian stewardship. I thank God for those of you who have remembered [insert name of church] in your wills. Your faithful stewardship in planning for your death has strengthened our parish immeasurably.

Bibliography

Ad Hoc Committee on Stewardship. *Stewardship, a Disciple's Response to the U.S. Bishops Pastoral Letter on Stewardship.* Washington, D.C.: National Conference of Catholic Bishops, February, 1997.

Callahan, Kennon. *Giving and Stewardship in an Effective Church.* New York: Harper Collins, 1992.

Foster, Richard. *The Challenge of the Disciplined Life: Christian Reflections on Money, Sex, and Power.* New York: Harper Collins, 1985.

Hueckel, Sharon. *Stewardship by the Book.* Kansas City, Mo.: Sheed & Ward, 1996.

"Life of the Christian Steward—A Reflection on the Logic of Commitment." A Booklet. Washington, D.C., International Catholic Stewardship Council.

Madden, Mary Roger. *Gladly Will I Spend and Be Spent.* Washington, D.C.; N.C.S.C., 1997.

New American Bible with Revised New Testament. Washington, D.C.: Confraternity of Christian Doctrine, Inc., 1986.

"Stewardship for Global Solidarity; a Report on the Second International Seminar in Rome, Italy, December, 1998." *Resource Journal* VIII. Washington, D.C.: International Catholic Stewardship Council, 1999.

Quotation from *Soul and Money: A Theology of Wealth.* W. Taylor Stevenson, used by permission of the Office of Stewardship of the Episcopal Church Center.

The poem "The Bustle in the House, from *The Complete Poems of Emily Dickinson,* edited by Thomas H. Johnson, published by Little, Brown and Company. Used by permission.

Excerpts from the poems "The Leaden Echo" and "The Golden Echo" by Gerald Manley Hopkins from *Poems in Prose,* selected and edited by W. H. Gardner, published by Oxford University Press. Used by permission.

Contributors

Georgia Anderson, Director of Planned Giving, Catholic Church Extension Society, Chicago (SO-12, SO-13)

Greg Bowden, Director of Annual Appeal, Diocese of Charleston (SO-77)

Rev. Msgr. Joseph M. Champlin, Rector, Cathedral of the Immaculate Conception, Syracuse, New York (G-26, G-30)

The Rev. Phoebe L. Coe, Pastor, Church of the Epiphany, Odenton, Maryland (SO-41, S0-42)

Catherine Coghlan, Office of Stewardship and Development, Archdiocese of Kansas City in Kansas (CY-22, CY-23)

The Rev. Roy A. Cole, Specialist for Revitalization, Baltimore (G-24, G-25, G-27, G-29, G-31)

Canon W. David Crockett, Episcopal Diocese of Western Massachusetts, Springfield (CY-24, G-19, G-20, G-21)

Chris Deets, Basilica of St. Mary, Minneapolis (G-6, G-13)

Dr. Leonard DeFiore, President, National Catholic Education Association, Washington, D.C. (SO-14, SO-15)

Sandy Ferencz, Director of Stewardship and Development, Diocese of Charleston (G-14, SO-70)

Dr. Elinor R. Ford, Fairview, North Carolina (SO-74, SO-75)

Dr. Amelia J. Geary, Director, Center for Teaching, Virginia Theological Seminary, Alexandria (SO-5, SO-16)

Most Rev. Eugene J. Gerber, Bishop of Wichita (SO-72, SO-73)

Most Rev. Marcel Gervais, Archbishop of Ottawa (SO-39, SO-40, SO-62, SO-63)

Michael J. Gorman, Ph.D., Dean, Ecumenical Institute of Theology, St. Mary's Seminary, Baltimore (SO-80, SO-81, SO-82)

Sr. Rose Marie Hennessy, O.P., Mission San Jose, California (SO-17)

Sharon Hueckel, Director, Pastoral Office for Development, Diocese of Lafayette in Indiana (CY-20, SO-59)

The Rt. Rev. Robert Ihloff, Episcopal Bishop of Maryland, Baltimore (CY-11, CY-15)

Rev. Fred Kammer, S.J., President, Catholic Charities of the U.S.A., Alexandria, Virginia (SO-11)

His Eminence William Cardinal Keeler, Archbishop of Baltimore (SO-55)

Most Rev. James Keleher, Archbishop of Kansas City in Kansas (CY-6, SO-43)

The Rt. Rev. C. L. Longest, Episcopal Suffragan Bishop of Maryland, Baltimore (SO-71, SO-84)

Rev. James V. Matthews, St. Benedict Church, Oakland, California (CY-9, CY-21)

Rev. Msgr. Thomas McGread, Pastor, St. Francis of Assisi Church, Wichita (SO-78)

The Rev. Mary Morgan, Pastor, Maryland Presbyterian Church, U.S.A., Towson, Maryland (SO-45)

Most Rev. Robert F. Morneau, Auxiliary Bishop of Green Bay (G-2, G-22, G-32)

Fred Osborn, Director of Planned Giving, Episcopal Church Foundation, New York City (SO-49, SO-50, SO-51, SO-52, SO-53)

Matthew R. Paratore, Secretary General, International Catholic Stewardship Council, Inc., Washington, D.C. (CY-2, CY-3, CY-4, CY-5)

Most Rev. Ricardo Ramirez, C.S.B., Bishop of Las Cruces (SO-29, SO-30)

The Rev. Ronald L. Reed, Pastor, St. James Episcopal Church, Wichita (CY-27, SO-24, SO-44)

Catherine A. Ritter, Director of Family Life, Towson United Methodist Church, Towson, Maryland (SO-85)

Most Rev. Sylvester D. Ryan, Bishop of Monterey (CY-13, SO-25)

Francis "Dutch" Scholtz, Director, Office of Stewardship, Diocese of St. Augustine (G-23, G-28)

Andrew A. Simone, M.D., Executive Director, Canadian Food for Children (La Nourriture du Canada les Enfants), Toronto (SO-64, SO-65)

Terence T. Thompson, Director of Stewardship and Development, Archdiocese of Toronto (SO-68, SO-69)

Rev. Robert Vitillo, Executive Director, Catholic Campaign for Human Development, Washington, D.C. (SO-9, SO-10)

Rev. Francis W. Wright, C.S.Sp., National Director, Holy Childhood Association, Washington, D.C. (CY-25, SO-18)

The Rev. Tim Wright, Executive Pastor, Community Church of Joy, Phoenix (SO-60, SO-61)

Cross References
of Scripture Citations

Matthew

Mark

Indices

Church Year

General Sermons

Special Occasions